HOUSE ARREST:

**A Search for American Character
In and Around the White House,
Past and Present**

BY ANNA DEAVERE SMITH

DRAMATISTS
PLAY SERVICE
INC.

This play is dedicated to the following actors who performed it in another version at the Mark Taper Forum in the Spring of 1999.

Regina Carter (performer, composer and violinist)
Chad L. Coleman
Lynette Du Pre
Glenn Fleshler
Crispin Freeman
Francesca Harper
Ezra Knight
Linda Marie Larson
Kimber Riddle
Michele Shay
Eric Steinberg
Bahni Turpin

And to Gordon Davidson,

And to Congressman Amory and Mrs. Priscilla Houghton,

And to David Chalian, who took care of the 500 interviews upon which the project is based.

Special thanks to Douglas Wager, Riley Temple, Stephen Richard and the Arena Stage Theater.

GENERAL PRODUCTION NOTES

This is a form of documentary theater. It requires a different kind of acting than psychological realism, and depends on an "informed actor."

This play is about real events, using the words of real people. The audience should be made aware of that. Slides should be used, if possible, to announce each character, and to inform the audience that the words in the play are verbatim from interviews. A slide with the following language should begin the show, just after lights down, and before any other visual image:

"All words spoken by speakers in the 20th century are verbatim from interviews conducted by Anna Deavere Smith, unless otherwise noted. All other materials are verbatim from historic texts."

The audience also needs to be given a background on the events. This can be achieved by the use of dramaturgical notes, but it can also be included in the body of the play — with visual aids, such as slides and videos if possible. The overall context of the play is the Clinton Administration and the relationship of President Clinton to the press.

The actor's accuracy of language is important. All of the utterances, every "uh" and other non-verbal sounds where noted, are rhythmic beats which inform the development of character. Many times a character speaks in a counterintuitive way, in which words in and of themselves do not make sense. The play has been written as an extension of research done by the author on the relationship of language to identity. It is recommended that a specific person be included on the production team who gives line notes and makes corrections. The process of playing the play and speaking the words in their exact presentation is the core of the technique of performing the play.

Music and sound effects are useful and important for flow. In all initial productions, original music was composed.

Costumes, stage sets and props can be as minimal or as ornate as one imagines. The play is performed in bare feet, except when shoes are meant to make a specific statement.

The play sees actors as cultural workers, who reach towards that which is "other" than themselves, to reach towards that which is different from themselves. To this extent, typecasting should only be used in relationship to casting which is about that reach for the other. People can be cast across race, age and gender lines. The play is vocally and verbally demanding, and requires first and foremost actors with a good vocal and physical range and a facility with language and movement.

HOUSE ARREST was produced by the Public Theater (George C. Wolfe, Producer; Rosemarie Tichler, Artistic Producer; Mark Litvin, Managing Director) in New York City on March 26, 2000. The directorial consultant was Jo Bonney; the set design was by Richard Hoover; the lighting design was by Kevin Adams; the costume design was by Ann Hould-Ward; the sound design was by Ken Travis; the projection design was by Batwin & Robin Productions; the composer was Julia Wolfe; the production dramaturg was Mervin P. Antonio; and the production stage manager was James Latus. It was performed by Anna Deavere Smith.

CHARACTERS

Eleven of the characters are people who are alive, or who were alive. They can be played by a company of one or more actors. Actors play several different roles. Gender and race do not need to match that of the character listed.

STUDS TERKEL

GEORGE STEPHANOPOULOS

CINDER STANTON

PENNY KISER

KEN BURNS

JAMES CALLENDER

THOMAS JEFFERSON

ROGER KENNEDY

EUGENE FOSTER

RW APPLE

LIZZIE MCDUFFIE

WALTER TROHAN

MICHAEL K. FRISBY

GARY HART

PEGGY NOONAN

ELIZABETH KECKLEY

PRESIDENT ABRAHAM
LINCOLN

WALT WHITMAN

BEN BRADLEE

BRIAN PALMER

GLORIA STEINEM

GOV. ANN RICHARDS

ALICE WATERS

GRAYDON CARTER

ANONYMOUS MAN

JUDITH BUTLER

ANITA HILL

ALEXIS HERMAN

MAGGIE WILLIAMS

ED BRADLEY

CHRISTOPHER HITCHENS

WALTER SHAPIRO

DAVID KENDALL

MIKE ISIKOFF

CHRIS VLASTO

PRESIDENT WILLIAM J.
CLINTON

PRESIDENT GEORGE
BUSH, SR.

FLIP BENHAM

CHERYL MILLS

PAULETTE JENKINS

BLESE CANTY

TABLE OF CONTENTS

ACT ONE

STUDS TERKEL — Clowns   13

GEORGE STEPHANOPOULOS — The Deal   18

I. COHABITATION: A VISIT TO JEFFERSON'S HOME AT MONTICELLO   20

CINDER STANTON — Pantops   20

PENNY KISER — Justice is in One Scale   22

KEN BURNS — James Callender   24

JAMES CALLENDER — The Recorder Newspaper, 1803   25

ROGER KENNEDY — Unconsummated Affections/Deep Denial   26

CINDER STANTON — On Sally Hemings   30

SCIENTIFIC EVIDENCE 1781–1998   31

THOMAS JEFFERSON   33

ROGER KENNEDY — Could Have Not Had Our Mess as Bad   34

EUGENE FOSTER — Probability   36

KEN BURNS — Tea Cup   38

II. AN EASIER TIME   40

RW APPLE — At All, At All, At All, At All   40

WALTER TROHAN — An Easier Time   42

LIZZIE McDUFFIE — Canary Bird   43

WALTER TROHAN — How Could I Say   47

MICHAEL K. FRISBY —Bowling   49

LIZZIE McDUFFIE — Hot Water Bottle/Peeved   52

GARY HART — Look in Windows   54

PEGGY NOONAN — Asylum   56

III. THE GRAND DEATHS OF THE RACE   58

ELIZABETH KECKLEY   58

PRESIDENT ABRAHAM LINCOLN — Lincoln's Dream   60

BRIAN PALMER — Body Watch   62

WALT WHITMAN — President of the United States   64

BEN BRADLEE — Performers   66

BRIAN PALMER — Political Theater   69

GLORIA STEINEM — Three Murders   71

GOV. ANN RICHARDS — Birds That were Loose   72

ACT TWO

I. BIT BY BIT, DROP BY DROP — 79
ALICE WATERS — Presidential Peach — 79
GRAYDON CARTER — Well She was Just Great — 82
ANONYMOUS MAN — Lambs to Dinner — 83
GRAYDON CARTER — Didn't Bother Me — 84
JUDITH BUTLER — A Scream — 85
ANONYMOUS MAN — Way Too Academic — 86
GRAYDON CARTER — That Arc — 88

II. SENDING THE CANARIES INTO THE MINES — 90
ANITA HILL — Slick, Dirty — 90
MAGGIE WILLIAMS — Lie Detecting — 91
ALEXIS HERMAN — Washington Political Insider — 92
MAGGIE WILLIAMS — Making a Kind of a Political Point — 100
ANITA HILL — House Arrest — 102

III. DARKNESS AT NOON — 104
ED BRADLEY — Captives — 104
CHRISTOPHER HITCHENS — Sex and Death — 107
WALTER SHAPIRO — Are You Now or Have You Ever Been? — 110
DAVID KENDALL — Is Is — 112
WALTER SHAPIRO — Spinach Dip/Sad — 114
MIKE ISIKOFF — Persistence — 115
CHRIS VLASTO — The Blue Dress — 117

IV. POLITICAL THEATER — 118
PRESIDENT WILLIAM J. CLINTON — Baby Huey — 120

V. MORAL SLIPPAGE — 124
PRESIDENT GEORGE BUSH, SR. — Fat, Dumb and Happy — 124
FLIP BENHAM — Does a Tree Make a Sound? — 126
CHERYL MILLS — A Baby Face Down in the Water — 129
PAULETTE JENKINS — Mirror to Her Mouth — 130
BRIAN PALMER — Getting Beaten Up in an Alley — 134

VI. ONE CARD AT A TIME — 136
BLESE CANTY — Right by the Rope — 136
STUDS TERKEL — Communication — 138

HOUSE ARREST

ACT ONE

SLIDE AT BEGINNING OF PLAY

All words spoken by speakers in the 20th century are verbatim from interviews conducted by Anna Deavere Smith, unless otherwise noted. All other materials are verbatim from historic texts.

Studs Terkel

CLOWNS

Ya know, when it gets back to as far as guys,
Presidents with dames —
My God!
Ya know!
Kennedy, my God!
It wasn't so much Addison's disease,
he suffered from Satyriasis probably!
In fact he said it!
So what?
And my favorite President,
the one
the one President of the century,
major league,
FDR of course,
well FDR is said to have had a fling with a socialite!
And he had polio!
I said my God the man has polio,
this might be very good therapy!
Long before McCarthy there was New Salem.
I think Hillary has a point —
about it being a right wing ...
(But.)
that's too simple!
Well of course they're out to get him!
That's not what the issue is to me!
The issue is —
What the hell have we learned?
Where are we?
I was born in 1912,
the year the Titanic,
sank —

the greatest ship ever built —
It hits the tip of an iceberg and bam! It went down.
It went down,
and I came up,
Wow some century!
ANNA DEAVERE SMITH V.O. What's the defining moment in
American History?
STUDS TERKEL. Defining moment in American History?
I don't think there's one
you can't say Hiroshima
That's a big moment
I don't think there's any one
I can't pick out any one
It's a combination of many
I can't think of any one moment I'd say is the defining moment,
But the gradual slippage
slippage is the word used by people in
Watergate
moral slippage,
It's a gradual kind of thing
A combination of things.
But it's not this —
this almost becomes not the crowning touch,
but the clowning touch!
It's the clowning touch!
It ends with a fright wig,
putty nose,
with baggy pants!
And this is it!
It's not just Clinton and Monica!
We all are wearing the fright wig and putty nose and baggy pants!
We're all demeaned!
By that, I mean,
all of us are clowns and that's what its all about!
Instead of a new century
with all the discoveries made,
in medicine —
perhaps more to come

and yet with fewer and fewer people controlling,
more and more and more,
and the more and more and more feeling more and more and more
helpless.
And who *runs* the means of communication that condition these
people to vote as
they vote and think as they think?
We got Lewinsky-ism and Monica-ism!
Instead of "what the hell we been doing to all these countries and
to the have
nots in this country?"
So we're wearing baggy pants, putty nose, and
fright wigs.
We've been *conditioned* to wear them
by this time.
(Pause.)
We've-got-to-question-official-truth!
The thing that was so great about Mark Twain!
We honor Mark Twain ya know —
but we don't *read* 'im!
We may read *Huck Finn* —
Eeven Huck of course was tremendous.
Remember what Huck did?
That great scene on the raft you know —
when Huck
see —
You have to
question official truth!
So truth is the *law* was
A black man is *property* is a *thing!*
And he's *(Huck is.)* on with a property named Jim,
a slave, see —
on the raft —
and he heard that Jim says he's going to do a terrible *thing*
And Huck is thirteen, twelve
and Jim said he's going to look for his wife and kids
and he's gonna *steal* them
from the woman

or person who *owns* them
and Huck says "That woman never did me any harm!
(Whispering.)
I'm —
he's gonna *steal!*
In in Huck's own mind —
Huck Finn is what it's all about —
the goodness of Huck, you see —
He's an illiterate kid right?
He's had no schoolin' —
But there's something in 'im. *(Whispering, expressive, urgent.)*
And he says "Oh it's a terrible thing, wow what an awful thing he's
gonna *steal."*
And just then
Two slavers caught up!
the guys chasing the slaves —
lookin' for Jim
ya know
and they come up "Anybody on that raft with ya?"
(Pause.)
And Huck yeah (dibdebi)
(They know there's somebody there. Pause.)
"Is he white or black?"
And Huck says
(Pause.)
"White."
and they go off
"Oh my God my conscience"
"I lied!"
Ya know
I lied
and he's gonna —
but if
"I did a terrible thing"
(Pause.)
"Why do I feel so *good?"*
There ya got it!
in Huck

ya captured the human species
That stuff that Huck is there
that part's been buried!

Slide: George Stephanopoulos, Former Assistant to President Clinton

"THE DEAL"

Sipping a Martini.

We're a celebrity culture,
and the President is the Celebrity-in-Chief.
I think the only private time a President has,
is when he's in the Oval —
and he walks from the Oval
to either his private study or his private bathroom.
That's it!
Once he's in the residence he can move *between* rooms
But there's still some servants around.
As far as officially, the only truly private time he has is within that small suite,
which is one
(He counts.)
It's four rooms, plus a terrace and one of those rooms is a bathroom.
He's sitting at a desk with one of the best views in Washington —
certainly the best morning light I've ever seen in my life —
But it's got glass this thick,
that can't be
touched.
You've got a
two secretaries on the outside,
and two Secret Service people between them —
as you move *across* the hall *in* the Oval
there's another room to where,
there's a tiny little pantry and there's another Secret Service agent there —
And then you get to *my* office

And-every-door —
is wired!
Like if I
moved in the back door,
between my office and the Oval
the secret service would know! Because it was wired!
And —
I've never thought of it this way before —
What happens, when you juxtapose incredible, immense, power —
but the price —
I mean it's a different
Um,
It's a different devil's choice!
The price is,
Transparency.
Everything you do is known.
You can be the most *powerful* person in the world *(Upward inflection.)*
You're going to uh,
have every privilege known to man!
Every whim is going to be catered to!
the deal is —
You can do whatever you want.
The price is that everybody is going to know
everything you do.

I. COHABITATION: A VISIT TO JEFFERSON'S HOME AT MONTICELLO

Cinder Stanton, Historian at Monticello

"PANTOPS"

Cinder is centerstage on a stool.

Uh.
So
I'm reading something this morning talking about Jefferson
as a landscape designer
and he uses the word "Panoptic" uh
which means
all seeing uh.
It can also mean
all *seen* from everywhere
Which is interesting.
It's one of those Greek words that uh,
because
Jefferson had named one of his farms
"Pantops" you know based on that,
which means
either seen from everywhere,
or you can see everything *from* there
Um,
so the whole choice,
of Monticello as a panoptic,
uh perch,
basically
is very very
Jeffersonian.

(Pause.)
He certainly took measures so that he couldn't *be* seen.
But
he bought everything he could see,
and then a hundred yards beyond the line of sight.
So it was obvious,
he was just sort of buying his own
view,
there.
It's interesting, just in relation to what you said in terms of modern
Presidents.
That that word has a double meaning.
That they are all-seeing,
or being seen by everyone.

"JUSTICE IS IN ONE SCALE"

Okay. Okay, he couldn't take care of it. What, what-what, what's another reason? Those are good reasons. What else do you think? What else? *(Laugh.)*

Thinking he never learned, right. That he was just a big boss? He was. Yeah, he was. Most people say, well, economically, he couldn't afford it. And that is true. You know, he died a hundred seven thousand dollars in debt. Many of his slaves were mortgaged, so he didn't have the right to sell them, but, oh I mean to free them, but also, Thomas Jefferson said, he said, "You know, to free people brought up in the habits of slavery is like abandoning children."

Remember that law of 1806? When they had to leave within a year? That, uh played a big part in his decision, too. He just said until America is ready, these slaves can't be free. We all have to agree. You know, in his notes on the State of Virginia — now some of us might say, well, that's kind of a cop-out by Thomas Jefferson, but in his notes on the State of Virginia, he had a plan, and his plan was ... eh, I think he sort of set the year, December 31, 1800, he said, let's everybody ... He said, by then, this is the age of the Enlightenment, everybody will agree slavery is wrong, and by that year, let's take all the new babies born that year, we're gonna separate 'em from their mother and father. He said, I know that's gonna be hard, but, we've got to do it. And he said, the government's gonna pay. And we're going to train them, according, he said, to their genius. In trades. Then, when the women reach eighteen and the men twenty-one, we're going to take them, lock, stock, and barrel, and place them in a black community, maybe in the West Indies. Or maybe back to Africa. 'Cause he said, um, they will never forgive us for what ha — the, the way we treated them.

So, we will start trading. They, they'll have their own little country, we'll pay until they're ready. Okay, that was his plan. He was so disappointed when he, by 1800, you know, nobody's ready to do it. One of his friends, Edmund Coves, writes him, and he says, Now listen, I'm leavin' Virginia, and I'm freeing my slaves, and you ought to be the example. You ought to do the same thing. He said, No. He said, I'm so sorry you have to leave Virginia. But he said, I just cannot abandon, you know, my family. He knew the time would come, and he felt that eventually everyone would agree, but until that time came, he said I wouldn't do it.

But, you know, too, the first forty years of his life, he speaks out against slavery. The last forty years, he gets real quiet.

Also (Thomas Jefferson) said about the slaves, he said, "Justice is in one scale and self-preservation in the other."

Now, one thing Abraham Lincoln said, that sort of clears it up a little bit for me, 'cause I get kind of mad at Thomas Jefferson, you know, for not being the example, but Abraham Lincoln said, "All praise to Jefferson." Cause he said, in the Declaration, Thomas Jefferson said, "Life, Liberty, and the Pursuit of Happiness," and he didn't put the word "property" in there?

Abraham Lincoln said if he had "property," and Thomas Jefferson knew this, if he had put that word "property" in, that Abraham Lincoln wouldn't have had this document that says, legally, "All-men-are-created-equal." You know, therefore, they should be free. And he said, "Because of Thomas Jefferson's foresight ... "

Any questions about that?

Ken Burns, Filmmaker

"JAMES CALLENDER"

Ken Burns is seated in a rocking chair.

You know what the Sally Hemings story is about?
Jefferson, hired newspapermen —
He said to Madison
"Hire people, who will *savage* Hamilton and Adams without let up
to *savage* them in the newspapers.
Callender, who was an alcoholic
(which is not a condition unfamiliar with those in our nation's
Capital)
turned *against* Jefferson
and wrote in a *Federalist* newspaper
his story about Sally Hemings.
No one's ever proved it no one's ever disproved it.

James Callender, Journalist

"THE RECORDER NEWSPAPER, 1803"

Callender is at a 19th-century writing desk, writing by candlelight, in a vest and drinking from a bottle. He speaks with a thick Scottish brogue.

It is well known, that the man, whom it delighteth the people to honor, keeps and for many years past has kept, as his concubine, one of his own slaves.

Her name is Sally. The name of her eldest son is *Tom*. The boy is ten or twelve years of age. His features are said to bear a striking (although sable) resemblance to those of the President himself.

Other information assures us that Mr. Jefferson's Sally and her children are real persons, that the woman herself has a *room* to herself in Monticello in the character of seamstress to the family, if not as housekeeper; that she is industrious and orderly in her behavior, but that her intimacy with her master is well known. *(Callender puts on a skirt, that is Sally Hemings' skirt, drinks, sings, and dances. Sings to the tune of "Yankee Doodle.")*

Of all the damsels in the green
on Mountain or in valley,
A lass so luscious ne'er was seen,
As Monticellan Sally!

You call her slave, and pray were slaves
Made only for the galley?
Try for yourselves, ye witless knaves,
And take to be your Sally.

Slide: Roger Kennedy, Scholar

"UNCONSUMMATED AFFECTIONS/DEEP DENIAL"

A constructed dialogue: These people said these words but not in each other's presence.

This should be played by one person who goes back and forth between Kennedy and Reed.

Kennedy/Reed crosses centerstage and sits on stool for the following debate. Kennedy with a coffee cup and Reed with a mimosa.

I think Jefferson wasn't,
I think Jefferson,
as a man of words and unconsummated
a — ffections,
Ah,
there's just
not a *shred,*
not a *shred* of evidence
**(Slide: Annette Gordon Reed Legal Scholar and Author of
"Sally Hemings")**
ANNETTE GORDON REED. Well that's crazy.
ROGER KENNEDY. That *before* his wife,
or *after* his wife there was anybody
with whom he was intimate
physically.
ANNETTE GORDON REED. Well that's crazy.
ROGER KENNEDY. I just think,
I I don't I don't think it's necessary.
ANNETTE GORDON REED. That's not true.
That's the asexual idea.
That is just — un-true.

26

And when somebody says something like that they can say the evidence doesn't convince them,
but to say there's no evidence,
that person is,
not a shred,
in deep denial.
And that person has to sit back
and think,
what is it about
this story that bothers you because you're not dealing realistically with it.
"There's not a shred."
It may not be enough to convince people, it's enough to convince me,
it would convince people about any other guy in the world,
any other slave owner in the world,
it would be no question about it,
with what I've presented,
you can say it's not enough to convince you
but to say there's not a shred of evidence is just wrong, it's just flat
— wrong.
ROGER KENNEDY. Here are the signs and signals:
That there is this succession of young men
(quite handsome all of them),
that were his secretaries,
a gay friend of mine thinks this is *terribly* exciting.
ANNETTE GORDON REED. I haven't seen it written anywhere,
but there's a suggestion that
well
maybe.
maybe he was gay.
Maybe,
that's why he,
never got married again
after
his wife died.
And I was joking with someone about this

27

I said, it's sort of like
pick your nightmare,
for historians.
I mean it's like if there's any intimation that he was *gay*
Somebody will pick up the Sally Hemings story just like that.
(Snapping her fingers.)
Oh but she was the love of his life,
it's like which is worse to be involved with a black woman or be gay?
The problem with the gay angle is, as I say —
if you don't have something
any indication that he had —
sex with
men,
but we need a name or an instance or something that indicates that
before you can have that as a realistic alternative
to this.
You see what I'm saying?
ROGER KENNEDY. I don't care, in a sense.
He surrounded himself with beautiful people.
Mostly male cause that's safe!
And where the hell are you gonna get a beautiful female to have
around if you're not married to her in Virginia?
ANNETTE GORDON REED. I mean anything is possible
the other thing is,
that he masturbated.
Some people say well how do you know he wasn't just masturbating
all this time.
That that's how he,
I mean there are any number of
I mean he could have been doing anything —
Masturbating,
there are people who thought he just masturbated and that's how he
people have said this
people talk about it.
Historians surmise that.
ROGER KENNEDY. I think it's
only *sad*
Because the chances that they ever got anywhere

together
are just
zero
No,
I just think he was
in *love*
I mean he was *lonesome*
I mean we all get *lonesome*
ANNETTE GORDON REED. This is a story
about a family of people
whether it's Jefferson or not
and these people were shut out of that family
because of
race. *(Sally's rocker is being lit while Anna Deavere Smith is changing for Jefferson.)*

Slide: Cinder Stanton, Historian at Monticello

"ON SALLY HEMINGS"

Anna Deavere Smith's voice is heard. (In the original production, the actual tape of the interview was used. Here a tape could be created with actors.)

ANNA DEAVERE SMITH V.O. And then again I mean we have no doc ... there are no documents from her am I right about that?
CINDER STANTON. Right, nothing.
ANNA DEAVERE SMITH. Nothing at all?
CINDER STANTON. Nothing at all. No image, no documents.
ANNA DEAVERE SMITH. Was she literate — do we know that?
CINDER STANTON. We don't even know that. We know that, um ...
ANNA DEAVERE SMITH. She could speak French though, right? They taught her to speak French.
CINDER STANTON. Well, we — it's an assumption. There's no record that she was given lessons, there's no record that, um, she knew it but you know it's a pretty strong assumption.

SCIENTIFIC EVIDENCE 1781–1998

From the notes on the state of Virginia.

A blackboard is brought on stage. Jefferson dons a beautiful 18th-century waistcoat and asks for two crew members (one white, one black) to come on stage to assist his demonstration.

JEFFERSON. The first difference which strikes us is that of colour. Whether the black of the Negro resides in the reticular membrane between the skin and the scarf skin, or in the scarf skin itself, whether it proceeds from the colour of the bile, or from that of some other secretion, the difference is fixed in nature.
Are not the fine mixtures of red and white,
preferable to that eternal monotony, that immovable veil of black which covers all the motions of the other race?
They have less hair on the face and body.
They secrete less by the kidneys and more by the glands of the skin, which gives them a very strong and disagreeable odor. They are more ardent after their female,
but love seems with them to be a more eager desire, than a tender delicate mixture of sentiment and sensation.
In general, their existence appears to participate more of sensation than reflection.
Comparing them with their faculties of memory they are equal to whites, in reason much inferior,
and in imagination they are dull, tasteless and anomalous.
Never could I find that a black had uttered a thought above the level of plain narration.
Their inferiority is not the effect merely of their condition of life. I advance it therefore as a suspicion only, that the blacks whether originally a distinct race, or made distinct by time and circumstances, are inferior to the whites in the endowments of body and mind.
This unfortunate difference of colour, and perhaps of faculty is a

powerful obstacle to the emancipation of these people.
When freed he is to be removed beyond the reach of mixture.
(Jefferson approaches the blackboard and writes on it.)

FROM CORRESPONDENCE OF
THOMAS JEFFERSON

JEFFERSON. You asked me in conversation, what constituted a mulatto by our law?

It becomes a mathematical problem.

Let the first crossing be of *a,* pure Negro, with A, pure white. The unit of blood of the issue being composed of the half of that of each parent, will be a/two + A/two. Call it, for abbreviation, b (half blood).

Let q and e cohabit, the half of the blood of each will be q/two + e/two = a/eight + A/eight + B/four + a/sixteen + A/sixteen + B/eight + C/four = a(3)/sixteen + A(3)/sixteen + B(3)/eight +C/four, wherein 3/sixteen of a is no longer a mulatto. Our canon considers two crosses with the pure white, as clearing the issue of the Negro blood.

But observe, that this does not reestablish freedom, which depends on the condition of the mother. So much for this trifle by way of correction.

Roger Kennedy

"COULD HAVE NOT HAD OUR MESS AS BAD"

The cohabitation is palpable.
When you're in that bed
and in that room
and the
smell and *sound* of black people is absolutely the first thing that
hits you in the morning —
Every laugh,
Every salacious comment,
Every,
what you're having for breakfast,
It's right where that pond is!
Right there!
It's that close!
The guy serving your *tea*
is your
nephew
really.
That's, just
That's
That that that you can,
that's very *rough*
torture I think.
The obscenity is
that very few who got so interested in it
were interested in all those red-headed kids
running around Monticello.
Nobody paid any attention to *them*
Until they got interested in the possibility that
Mr. *Tom*
had produced a baby
with a black woman

when the place was *teeming* with kids
produced with black women.
We are talking about *scores*
of children produced in a power relationship.
He lived in a *swarm* of children conceived in power relationships,
that were unacceptable to any moral person.
Instead of being *mad* at him
which is easy,
this is somebody who lived
for a —
until eighty
knowing
that he was living everyday in moral ambiguity.
Everything he did, had a shadow side to it.
In 1806 there was a very large congressional debate about whether
slaves
were to go into the Louisiana Purchase or not
and Jefferson
who
who had done *nothing* since 1784
to make it harder for slavery to spread into the west
nothing
found it convenient not to have his acquisition free.
Everything after that Missouri and all the rest of it
flowed from a *failure* to
stop it when it could have been stopped.
It isn't true
that we didn't have another chance
So we could — have — not — had — our — mess
as bad.
Yeah.
To me *that's* the story.

"PROBABILITY"

Our uh,
scientific results did not prove,
that Thomas Jefferson
fathered any of Sally Hemings' children,
But that
the information that we got
taken in the context of the best available historical information
makes it extremely likely.
I think that the general public does not understand that.
I think that the general public uh has come to believe that
the DNA evidence
has proved the relationship
We absolutely cannot say that.
I emphasized strongly
and in a *loud* voice
I emphasized strongly
that it would not be possible
for us to prove
anything
with one hundred percent certainty
either positively or negatively
I have long understood
That the whole idea of probability is
something that most people just
don't understand.
If you say well this is very likely
uh,
that's something people don't want
to deal with.
They want to know is it or isn't it?

What one can say in summary is that this has tipped the weight of evidence very strongly in favor of the interpretation
that Thomas Jefferson
is more likely,
the father.

Slide: Ken Burns, Filmmaker

"TEA CUP"

Ken Burns is in the rocking chair stage right.

It doesn't matter.
He owned her.
Get the story straight.
I mean he could have killed her if he wanted.
He *owned* her!
He could have done anything with her!
He could have *murdered* her —
They could have said "Mr. President where's Sally?"
And he could have said "Oh I killed her last night, she displeased
me," and there wasn't a law in the land that
could have touched him.
The fact of whether he did or he didn't,
this late 20th century obsession with all things
sexual, titillating, and celebrity-driven is an anathema to historical truth.
He *owned* her and we forget that fact, but the fact that
the man-who-authored-the-world's-words-which-we-consider-
our-*creed*
held in chattel slavery more than two hundred human beings
one of whom
was a young, and we are told attractive and potentially lover for
him, but it doesn't matter the sexual politics are overwhelmed
by the fact that he *owned* her!
I like the frisson that comes from
both sides —
"Yes of course he could have" but no he absolutely didn't!
But he *owned* her goddamn it
that's the point he *owned* her!
And that's what we forget —

And we go "yes yes yes"
I say "Okay
So can I tell you about slavery?"
I said
"Would you like to live
in a one room dirt floored shack fourteen by fourteen in which
you work fourteen hours a day — unless there is a full moon and
then you work more, you are not paid,
you can be beaten, you can be separated from your family. In fact
they changed the wedding vows for slaves to read "'Til death or
distance do you part." *(Slight pause.)*
You are susceptible to every known disease of which there is no
cure, you are denied the possibility of an education and in fact,
in many instances you would be punished for learning a language
or having a literature or having a culture,
Now tell me how long you would like to live under this?"
I would say a generation's too long.
A decade's too long, a year is too long.
A month is too long, a week's too long.
I submit if you were asked to do that
you might try it on for twenty minutes.
That's —
He *owned* her.
You know if I own you,
When I say he could have killed her —
You say
"Hell yes but he wouldn't have"
His-nephews-murdered-one-of-his-slaves
and their, that slave's crime had been to break a *tea cup* that had
belonged to their mother.
And there-was-no-recourse-in-the-United-States-of-America
He's both the blessing and the curse
As John Hope Franklin said
he insured, that we would inherit the poison of indecision on race.
And yet he also wrote us the prescription for the antidote.
For the serum that would cure us.
Jefferson said that slavery was like holding a wolf by the ears, you
didn't like it but you didn't dare let go.

II. AN EASIER TIME

Slide: RW Apple, Journalist — **The New York Times**

Sound: Restaurant Ambience, Laughter

"AT ALL, AT ALL, AT ALL, AT ALL"

Apple is in an Indian restaurant in Washington, D.C. near the White House, very upscale. He is drinking white wine. White linens and fine china are on the table, he wears a napkin at his neck and is eating Indian hors d'oeuvres. He is a large man, wearing a tie, blazer, penny-loafers, with a deep vocal register. He is surveying the menu with reading glasses.

But uh Roosevelt, Roosevelt conducted press conferences with reporters standing around his desk. But my God, what a change since — in the relatively short time between FDR and now. You know, the famous story about Bob Post? There was a reporter called Robert Post on the *New York Times* and who was later killed in a bombing raid over Williamshaben. I think — check it if you use it — during the war. But when he was a young reporter, and he came from a rather grand family like Roosevelt. And he asked an unanswer — an unanswerable question, an *unaskable* question to wit, "Are-you-going-to-run-for-a-third-term?" And Roosevelt said, *(Pronounced long and slow.)* "Bob, put your dunce cap on and go stand in the corner." Now, this is *not* something that would — could happen today, At all, at all, at all, at all! And there are no unaskable questions now as was demonstrated with the Gary Hart question in New Hampshire. Ya know you've just, you've gone from presuming what the President says is true and unthinking, unthinking backing of a war-time emergency, to presuming what the Presidents say is *un*true. And we've gone from credulousness, through what I would see as a relatively healthy period of of skepticism, to what I see now as a relatively *un*healthy period of cynicism. And what, what bothers me —

If I order — if I were to order the shrimp curry, could you make it a bit *hot?* So I won't — I need a bit of heat in this — in the hot weather. What you just — what do you think you'd like?

Walter Trohan, White House Correspondent for The Chicago Tribune from Presidents FDR–Nixon

"AN EASIER TIME"

Ninety-three years old, shuffling towards an easy chair, jacket and tie.

The only reason I'm talking to you to give you a feeling of a period
of an easier time
a friendlier time
When I had associations that reporters can't have today,
as I say
we were a family
We would have *parties* for Roosevelt and put on little shows for
'im
we'd sing songs and write little skits and so forth
We did different things and
he would —
Ohhhhhh
we'd pretend ta,
Oh *God,*
imitate Shirley Temple for example who was popular at that time
in uh
some silly song or other.
And he enjoyed that kind of nonsense.
And we'd have drinks of course …

Slide: *Voice of Bernard Asbell, Historian and Lizzie McDuffie, Former White House Cook for FDR*

"CANARY BIRD"

Bernard Asbell was a white man who interviewed Lizzie McDuffie in the fifties or sixties. He sounds like a fastidious historian who lives for details. Lizzie McDuffie, in reality, almost got cast as the role that Hattie McDaniel played in "Gone With the Wind," and sounds like it. She seems slightly intimidated by Asbell. Asbell's voice should be pre-recorded, or done on a God mike. (In the original production, the actual tape of Asbell was used. Here a tape could be created with actors.) He should not be seen. McDuffie is making biscuits.

VOICE OF BERNARD ASBELL. This is going to be an interview with Mrs. Lizzie McDuffie, and we've just started to talk right now. Do you recall, say on the morning of April twelfth ... maybe if I began with a question that I was wondering — *(Making biscuits center stage.)*
LIZZIE McDUFFIE. Yes, that will help me because uh
VOICE OF BERNARD ASBELL. Do you mind if I smoke a cigarette?
LIZZIE McDUFFIE. Oh no! Help yourself by all means.
VOICE OF BERNARD ASBELL. Do you know what he usually had — what — what do you, what would you guess he had on his breakfast tray that morning? Was there any —
LIZZIE McDUFFIE. Uh
well,
Mr. Roosevelt was very fond of fish.
he was a man that he like broiled fish.
He he liked — ed fish
he he ate well
And sometime he had scrambled eggs and bacon.

He liked bacon.
He always said that the bacon,
uh shouldn't,
couldn't use a knife and a fork with bacon and fried chicken.
You had to eat it with your fingers.
He said he always would
the bacon would fly off your plate and then you
you'd miss your bacon.
VOICE OF BERNARD ASBELL. Well now, as far as you can remember
on that morning,
uh the routine was as usual.
(Lizzie begins reading from her diary, unbound, handwritten sheets.)
That morning while I was getting the sitting room in order,
Mr. Roosevelt called to me and said
uh oh
Lizzie, Lizzie says uh
"You all were havin' a grand time this morning a grand time!"
And I said uh
"What do you mean Mr. Roosevelt?"
He said "Well, I heard all that laughter out there."
I said "Oh my, I wondered
did we disturb you?
I'm awful sorry."
"Oh no no no I enjoy
laughter he says
There's nothing in the world that fills me up like laughter," he said.
"The world needs more laughter."
And I said
"Well
you, do you
Mr. Roosevelt
are you um
do you believe in
oh what is that word?
Do you ...
(Lizzie looks on her paper.)

44

It's on here.

Do you do you

VOICE OF BERNARD ASBELL. That's alright …

LIZZIE McDUFFIE. *(She laughs.)*

I stammer so …

Do you believe in reincarnation?

VOICE OF BERNARD ASBELL. Oh! Reincarnation.

LIZZIE McDUFFIE. And he said

"Do I believe in what?"

I said "reincarnation."

He said "Do you believe in reincarnation?"

I said "I don't know whether I do or not I say" but I said "that's what Joe was trying to find out this morning.

Joe was the Filipino butler that we had carried down to help out with

us

uh on that trip.

And I says uh "He wants to know if I believe in reincarnation."

I said "I don't know whether I believe in it or not

but

in case there is such a thing as reincarnation

when I come back I want to be a canary bird."

He looked at me from head to foot and I weighed about two hundred pounds then

and he burst out into *peals* of laughter

And he had a favorite word that he always said when anything amused him

He said "Don't you love it don't you love it!??"

That was

VOICE OF BERNARD ASBELL. Whenever he was happy …

LIZZIE McDUFFIE. Oh yes.

Oh, that's the way he expressed himself.

Don't you love it? Don't you love it?!!!!

and I said,

"Well

(She takes more papers out of her apron pocket.)

I hope

I

will come back
and be a canary bird."
Then let's see what else
there was something else that was said
Oh goodness
I think after you are gone I'll think of everything.
Well ...

"HOW COULD I SAY"

Personally,
he was charming,
He had charisma.
But I didn't like his private life.
I must say
he brought his mistress into the White House
ANNA DEAVERE SMITH V.O. Why didn't anybody write
about that?
(Pause.)
WALTER TROHAN. ... because she was so nice
and if anybody mentioned it to me
and said she was the mistress and what not
I'd say
"You got a dirty mind." *(Pause. Considering.)*
She
was in
love with the guy
and she was a charming person
and she was crazy about him
I was sympathetic
toward her.
I didn't think it was the right thing for him to do *(Angrily.)*
and then he *disgusted* me completely
and I was very angry
(Privately.)
when
when he got playin' around with Crown Princess Margaret.
It broke (Missy's) heart
and she got very *ill*
went into Doctor's hospital
and Roosevelt

called on her *once!*
And ya know what he did?
He took his *wife* with him.
And I thought the *idea* of takin' the wife to see your *discarded mistress*
because you were *ashamed* to go in there alone
it rather disgusted me.
ANNA DEAVERE SMITH V.O. But you never wrote about it?
WALTER TROHAN. I *couldn't* (write) about it.
I couldn't say she was his mistress —
because she was in the White House as the secretary —
and everybody knew she was the mistress —
but how could you say it?
They could have *blasted* me and I would have been a terrible
character
Well I don't know
I don't think my paper would have printed it.
Actually, ya know he wasn't functioning for the last year or so
He was ill
I knew he was dyin',
his own doctor said he was healthy,
I knew there was
things were goin' on
so
I knew he was having doctors come in,
I was his, I tell ya I'm a reporter, and I
enlisted
got another reporter,
and the two of us brought a doctor
and sat him at a White House dinner,
White House Correspondents dinner
within a few feet of Roosevelt
to watch 'im and tell 'em how he was go what he thought of him
and then after the dinner
I said "Well how was he?"
He says "He's a dyin' man."

Michael K. Frisby, Journalist — The Wall Street Journal

"BOWLING"

And, now, fast forward into the White House. Okay?
George-Bush-is-always-inviting — now, I didn't
cover Bush,* but I heard stories. He'd invite reporters over
for little *chats.* He'd go *bowling,* bring them over for *bowling.*
Yeah, there's a bowling alley down in the White House:
He'd bring them over for — in the studio to see
movies with him and stuff. Okay?
Now, what I'll say is, I don't think that got him
favorable stories. Okay?
But what it *did* get him was benefit of the doubt.
Okay?
What I think that got him was when, whenever there was a issue
of, "Okay, who do I believe here? Do I believe George Bush? Or
do I believe somebody else?"
I think he got the benefit of the doubt from these
people because they knew him, they got to know him. *(Singsong.)*
They liked him.
I think they probably gave him the benefit of the doubt on some
things. Okay?
Bill Clinton *never* gets the benefit of the doubt because he has
kep'-us-at-such-a-distance.
Okay?
He has never let us in.
He has never let —
I mean I've,
I've gotten in by kind of prying and just,
you know,
making sure that I always keep my eye on this guy.
Okay?
That's how I've gotten to have a bit of an *understanding* with him.

* *Referring to George Bush Sr.*

Okay?

But he hasn't made it *easy,* because I'd get *rare* opportunities. *Okay?*

I think I've been to what?

I've been to like one dinner in the White House in five years?

I work for the *Wall Street Journal.*

Okay?

I've never been to the bowling alley.

Heh, heh.

Okay?

If he cuddled — if he cuddled up to us, he'd start getting benefit of the doubt.

Oh, I don't.

Look, look, look.

They may tell you that shit?

You going to tell me

that my colleagues wouldn't like to go bowling at the White House bowling alley with the President of the United States?

You going to tell me

that my colleagues wouldn't like to go over and see a movie with the President and the First Family?

Okay?

Now, not that I'm saying it would have any effect at all on news coverage.

Okay?

But if you were faced with a situation where you have to decide who you're going to believe, Bill Clinton or somebody else, and you've gotten to know this Bill Clinton a little bit and you suddenly start thinking that,

"Well, you know, he's got substance.

He's got a little more structure than I thought."

You might give him the benefit of the doubt!

That's where I think the President could benefit.

By the press knowing him a little more.

Okay.

And I'll tell you my personal?

I'm willing to bet that it would relate to a lot of other people.

Okay?

If I get a picture of me bowling with the President and I send that

to my mom or I send that to my aunts or I send that to my god-
mother, they're happy as all get-out, because when their friends
come to the house, they can say,
"Look!
There's Michael *bowling* with the President of the
United States."
Okay?

Slide: Lizzie McDuffie

"HOT WATER BOTTLE/PEEVED"

Reading from her sheets of paper, expressively, as if reading to a group of children.

When-I-asked-him-that-morning-how-he-felt
he says,
"I don't feel any ...
"I don't feel any too good this mornin'
Lizzie."
And he threw his hand right back there.
Just like that. *(She throws her hand back, imitating.)*
I was in the guest cottage
tidying up when Arthur came in and asked for a hot water bottle.
I got the hot, *(Uncertainly, unable to read her writing.)*
got the hot hot water bottle
and gave it gave it to him.
And in a few minutes Daisy came down and said "Lizzie, why
hadn't you come, why hadn't
you come down?" *(With emotion, as that person, very good perform-
ance.)*
And I said "It isn't the lunch is not ready yet.
It isn't lunch time!"
And I said "What happened?"
And she said "Oh Lizzie, I believe the President is dying." *(Very
good performance of that person, with feeling.)*
That was when I just *flew* to pieces!
That's when I said
"Why didn't you tell me?"
"Why didn't he tell me that the President was sick?"
and then I thought to myself —
Oh how much I loved him and how I waited on him all this time

and then Arthur would come *(Exasperated, angry.)*
and *know* he was sick
and wouldn't even tell me.
I was peeved about that
I remember having that, feeling like that about it.

Slide: Gary Hart, Candidate for President 1988

"LOOK IN WINDOWS"

I think it's much more profound than just
the press and people's private lives.
I think it's a real issue of control
I think what
political journalism in the late 20th century wants is control.
I think it wants to use its access,
its intrusiveness
to to control —
to have more control of the process,
political process.
And it also comes about in my case
For example saying when Hart was driven from the race.
I *wasn't* driven from the race.
I chose not to move forward.
It was *my* choice.
So that's the issue
What-is-the-meaning-of-language?
It's: what is the power, what is the control of the political process?
I think that's what the Gary Hart issue is about.
It wasn't about sex
or scandal.
It was about power.
Who-decides-who-will-run-for-office-in-this-country?
That's what it's about.
And who decides what is moral and immoral?
And how do you know what goes on in someone's house?
How do you know what goes on in someone's personal life?
You *can't.*
You *can't.*
That's-the-simple-point.
You can speculate.

You can spy.
You can look in the windows.
You can sensationalize.
You can use gossip.
But you will never,
never
know.

Peggy Noonan, Presidential Speechwriter for Presidents Reagan and Bush

"ASYLUM"

I'm not sure this is going to make any sense but since it may, let's try it.
You remember in the 18th century,
in the 18th and 19th century
in the finer and more refined circles in England
it became habit to go to um,
homes for the mentally ill and go see the people there and be very *moved* by their predicament?
It was a *weird*
sort of thing —
You wanted to go see the mad people and then feel.
Then I'm going to show all your friends
"See how compassionate I am."
I'm deeply *moved*
by their misery.
I am deeply *moved*
by the misery around me.
Then again I've always been very sensitive!
The-*press*-is-the-exact-opposite-of-that.
They they don't they want to go to the insane asylum and make the crazy people *cry!*
They want to go to the insane asylum with a fork and say, "Hey, how'd you like *that* Dole?" *(Makes a gesture: sticking the fork.)*
"Hey Clinton,
what did you mean about Susan McDougal and her
and her uh legal bills?"
I love to see old 1930's films of,
you know 1930's old tape
of the great ocean liner landing in New York and Greta Garbo gets off and you know says hello to her *fans?*

You know those old arrival
shipping news kind of videos from Movietone?
Do you remember the one with the Queen and King of England
coming down the *plank?*
And some some of the photographers start yelling, "Hey Queen
this way!"
That's what journalism is,
at its worst and still at its best!
"Hey-Queen-look-this-way,-hey-King-over-here"-click-click.

III. THE GRAND DEATHS
OF THE RACE

If done by one actor — wears Lincoln's shoes for all characters. Note on "The Grand Deaths of the Race": This section should feel like a kind of physical "jazz." If played by one actor, it should feel as though that actor were wandering through a variety of other people's dreams, or from one sideshow to the next at a carnival. Music should play behind the entire section. The play Our American Cousin *should have a sound design, which becomes more and more overpowering and grotesque as the act unfolds. The microphone should echo, or enhance, or distort Whitman from time to time. If more than one actor performs this section, it should seem that one actor flows to the next seamlessly — as if they are all disjointed parts of the same story. If more than one actor is used, the actor playing Lincoln should also play Palmer.*

Slide: The Lincoln White House

Slide: Elizabeth Keckley, Former Slave,
Dressmaker to Mrs. Lincoln

The stage is set up with a dressmaker's model stage left, a 19th-century coffin center stage, and Lincoln's rocker from Ford's Theater stage right.

ELIZABETH KECKLEY. My name is Elizabeth Keckley. My life has been an eventful one. I was born a slave — was the child of slave parents. The twelve hundred dollars with which I purchased the freedom of myself and son I consented to accept only as a loan. I went to work in earnest, and in a short time paid every cent. Ever since arriving in Washington I had a great desire to work for the ladies of the White House. One day when I was very busy, one of my patrons drove up to my apartments, came in where I engaged with my needle and said: "I know Mrs. Lincoln well, and you shall make a dress for her. It appears that Mrs. Lincoln had upset a cup of coffee on the dress.

I crossed the threshold of the White House for the first time. I became the regular dressmaker of Mrs. Lincoln. *(Music. A loud clock.)*

"LINCOLN'S DREAM"

From a letter written by Abraham Lincoln.

Sitting in a rocking chair, dressed in a long black coat and top-hat, using a microphone which should have some effect, as an echo, a reverb, etc. Music.

About ten days ago, I retired very late. I had been up waiting for important dispatches from the front. I could not have been long in bed when I fell into a slumber, for I was weary. I soon began to dream. There seemed to be a death-like stillness about me. Then I heard subdued sobs, as if a number of people were weeping. I thought I left my bed and wandered downstairs. There the silence was broken by the same pitiful sobbing, but the mourners were invisible. I went from room to room; no living person was in sight, but the same mournful sounds of distress met me as I passed along.

I saw light in all the rooms; every object was familiar to me; but where were all the people who were grieving as if their hearts would break? I was puzzled and alarmed. What could be the meaning of all this?

Determined to find the cause of a state of things so mysterious and so shocking, I kept on until I arrived at the East Room, which I entered.

There I met with a sickening surprise. Before me was a catafalque, on which rested a corpse wrapped in funeral vestments. Around it were stationed soldiers who were acting as guards; and there was a throng of people, gazing mournfully upon the corpse, whose face was covered, others weeping pitifully. "Who is dead in the White House?" I demanded of one of the soldiers, "The President," was his answer; "he was killed by an assassin."

Then came a loud burst of grief from the crowd, which woke me from my dream. I slept no more that night; and although it was only a dream, I have been strangely annoyed by it ever since.

"BODY WATCH"

"Stars and Stripes Forever" plays

Palmer in Lincoln's jacket and shoes, dons a baseball cap, on backwards.

Palmer, in reality a black man, crosses upstage of coffin to retrieve his photo bag, circles the stage with his light meter scoping the sight during the following speech. Palmer brings photo bag down left.

Like so many things in the journalistic realm these days
that's kind of market driven,
so
your competitors are there,
so you have to be there.
And if this cataclysmic event
actually does happen and your representative isn't there
to photograph it or to tape it, or to get first hand color
then um you're, you're, you're blown out of the water,
on
hour fifteen
of uh a Clinton
hour fifteen
of a Presidential trip to ya-know-*x*-state
When you're tromping through the thirty-seventh factory
of the day
and hearing the same boilerplate speech
it does feel a little bit like you're just there
to,

watch the body.
And see,
you know and and and to to to you know cover your organization
or *protect* (in the Washington lingo)
your organization in case
the unmentionable happens.
The unmentionable?
I mean just in case POTUS
gets you know POTUS gets *waxed.*
Oh right.
PRESIDENT-OF-THE-UNITED-STATES.

"PRESIDENT OF THE UNITED STATES"

1865. Whitman is standing stage right of coffin at a standing microphone with a bunch of lilacs in his hand. He is dressed like Lincoln, except no top hat.

The grand deaths of the race,
The dramatic deaths of every
nationality are its most
important inheritance — in some
respects beyond its literature
and art.
How often my heart has entertained the wish,
to give of Abraham Lincoln's death
its own special memorial.
The season being advanced,
there were many lilacs in full bloom. I find myself always
reminded of the great tragedy of that day by the sight and odor
of these blossoms.
The popular afternoon paper of Washington,
the little *"Evening Star,"*
had spattered all over its third page,
"THE PRESIDENT AND HIS LADY WILL BE AT THE
THEATRE THIS EVENING."
Lincoln was fond of the theatre.
I have myself seen him there several times.
I remember thinking how funny it was that he,
in some respects the leading actor in the stormiest drama known
to real history's stage through centuries,
should sit there and be so completely interested
and absorbed in those human jack straws,
moving about with their silly little gestures,

foreign spirit and flatulent text. *(Lincoln makes an entrance; as into Ford's Theater. Musical fanfare, ovation, applause, he bows and bows, as the shadow of Booth with a gun appears and the V.O. of the play begins.)*

Slide: From Our American Cousin, *a play performed at the Ford Theater in Washington the night Lincoln was shot*

MRS. M *(V.O. A woman's British voice.)* As to the state of your affections, remember, your happiness for life will depend on the choice you make.

AUG. *(V.O. A younger British woman's voice.)* What would you advise, mamma? You know I am always advised by you.

Ben Bradlee,* *Former Editor of* The Washington Post

"PERFORMERS"

In reality a white, patrician man in his seventies, handsome,
well heeled, perfect physical shape, sitting at a desk with a
swivel chair turned sideways.

Well, it started with television, right?
It started with television.
These guys,
uh — they were really performers uh, uh, Brinkley
uh,
Cronkite,
Severeid.
These were *performers* and uh, uh, it, it got so
that what they said
was less important than how they said it
and the authority that they could,
uh, force the public to believe they *had.*
And then as we got used to this,
as this became part of our *culture,*
they ceased to be reporters of any kind.
They're *not.*
But in this wonderful time
when we were downstairs in the city room,
when Hoffman was here,
Dustin,
And he was absorbing,
and trying to learn how we all talked
and what the culture of —

*Ben Bradlee was the editor of The Washington Post *when Watergate unfolded. The*
story broke on his watch. He is portrayed in "All the President's Men," by Jason
Robards

and, you know, not unlike what,
I guess, what you're doing.
And we got the word that there was a *jumper.*
A jumper means that somebody has gone out a window and is
threatening to jump into the street and off himself.
I said to Dustin,
Would you — yeah, you want to see this?
This is a,
uh, a kind of a, uh, ritual story.
Happens twice a year
and happens to almost all reporters.
They get to cover it.
So,
we went down and walked and it was right around the corner.
We walked a block and a half.
And, you know, everybody's looking *up* this way and a few people
say, "Jump, Jump!"
But mostly just looking.
Then they spotted Hoffman,
and the whole audience turned around and looked at *us.*
Just, they all looked at Hoffman!
Now, if, if,
uh, *Dan Rather* did that;
he went to cover a jump,
they'd do the same thing.
They *intrude* — *(Louder, stronger.)*
upon the event
and this is why the smart editors
who taught us wanted us off the stage
because, uh, uh, you *changed*
the event by your presence if you're really a performer.
There's a principle in physics
I have the book.
I bought this *huge* physics book
which is so unusual for me
called the *Heisenberg Principle*
and — and that is, if you,
if you, uh, split an atom,

you don't end up with two half-atoms; *(Louder.)*
you end up with two different things.
Observing the phenomenon *changes* the phenomenon.
WHITMAN. And so the figure Booth, the murderer ...

**Slide: The Booth/shadow appears. From Our American
Cousin, performed the night of Lincoln's death.
The melodrama below is very loud.**

MRS. M. Augusta my dear, to your room!
AUGUSTA. Yes, ma. the nasty beast.

Slide: Brian Palmer

"POLITICAL THEATER"

Palmer is loading film.

I hate to use a word as strong as "manipulation" but
essentially
I,
we are are are documenting political theater, I mean it's
it's
very elaborately staged political theater.
And it's the same under Republicans as it is under Democrats
They're trying to get their message out with as little
interference and as little noise as possible.
Having to
document that is kind of difficult.
I mean just sitting in the van,
the conversations that go on oftentimes
among photographers are often
about missed-pictures.
People who missed pictures.
So I mean you're ya know you're sort of really
imbued with this,
this knowledge from very early on.
Basically just like the Secret Service
you want to have the President *in* your viewfinder
or in your view
pretty much all the darn time.

Slide: Walt Whitman

Whitman is at the microphone.

And in the midst of the pandemonium, infuriated soldiers, the audience and the crowd, the stage, and all its actors and actresses, its paint pots, spangles and gas lights, the life blood from those veins, the best and sweetest of the land, drips slowly down and death's ooze already begins its little bubbles on the lips.

Slide: From **Our American Cousin,** *Performed the Night of Lincoln's Death.*

Lincoln sits and enjoys the play with laughter. The melodrama below is very loud, grotesque. The shadow of Booth gets bigger and bigger — gun is drawn slowly.

ASA. You crave affection, you do. Now I've no fortune, but I'm balling over with affections, which I'm ready to pour out all over you like apple sass, over roast pork.

MRS. M. I am aware, Mr. Trenchard, you are not used to the manners of good society, and that, alone, will excuse the impertinence of which you have been guilty.

ASA. Don't know the manners of good society, eh? Well I guess I know enough to turn you inside out old gal — you sockdoligizing old man trap. *(On "sockdoligizing old man trap," loud laughter on sound track of entire theater audience. Gunshot. Lincoln falls forward, hat rolls, actor morphs into Brian Palmer, if one actor, or if same actor plays Palmer as Lincoln and starts taking pictures madly. Strobe.)*

Gloria Steinem, Author/Activist

"THREE MURDERS"

Big chair comes on to center stage.

I always felt sorry for Nixon,
you know,
because he should not have been President.
And if it had not been for three murders,
he wouldn't have been.
(Pause.)
He was a classic example of —
Two Kennedys and a Martin Luther King,
I mean, on the grounds that I —
Well, because I think if he had not been —
because he was so much —
He and the movement were so much a bridge;
it was so focused on voting and the right to vote,
you know, and it was the bridge between —
a bridge between a giant populist movement for justice and the
system,
and when that bridge was gone,
I think it was very disillusioning and difficult.
But I don't mean to oversell, you know,
but it just — it always felt emotionally like it took three murders
to get him in office and he was clearly —
he had clearly risen to the level of his incompetence,
and he was a small man in a big office.
But every time I got
every time I felt sorry for him
he always did something so
horrendous
that then I would ...

Gov. Ann Richards, Former Governor of Texas

"BIRDS THAT WERE LOOSE"

Sitting in an elegant chair. (In reality a white woman in her sixties with beautiful white hair.) Texas accent.

I'm gonna get my coffee.
So you have the picture here —
The country uh
feels good because of this man who who because of his
ability to speak well,
because he conveyed a sort of new mission,
The problem was that he had his uh detractors.
I would say that a segment of the white population
whites and Hispanics
were
very enthusiastic about Jack Kennedy.
But the establishment
uh uh
No.
There was a very strong right wing movement
that we felt greatly in the state of Texas.
So when the decision was made for Kennedy,
When he made the decision was made to come to Texas
he was advised not-to-come.
Now, here's what was going on in Dallas.
There was a sort of a lunatic,
retired general
named Edwin Walker,
who lived out on Turtle Creek
that —
depending on what the Government did at one time or another
flew his flag upside down,

72

because that was a military sign of distress.
So the day that Jack Kennedy came to town
or maybe the week before,
I remember a lot of talk about the fact
that Edwin Walker was flying his flag upside down.
Uh
Lyndon and Lady Bird Johnson had come to visit Dallas —
They um were going into the downtown hotel and there were a
bunch of Republican women,
all dressed up
hats and gloves and the whole and
who were picketing
uh against Lyndon Johnson
and who
got carried away and *hit* Lady Bird,
and and Johnson
with their picket signs
Just stupid, silly
juvenile
embarrassing
kinds of stuff.
It wan' pretty.
It was grown up white boy games.
If you remember, in the old days,
Well of course you don't remember —
There was no Republican Party.
You couldn't participate
unless you were a Democrat.
So what you had in the Democratic party, were, Republicans.
So Kennedy made the decision he was going to come,
to try to heal-the-rift.
The luncheon was held in a place called the Apparel Mart —
Now this is,
this is interesting to me.
(She laughs.)
The Apparel Mart was a wholesale place,
and Dallas was really proud of it 'cause it was brand new,
with a big open atrium that went up about

four stories
and at that time I had about as much swat as a
fly swatter so
I think I was on the third balcony or something.
But here's the interesting thing —
in this hall there were,
parakeets.
Flying.
I mean,
Birds,
that were loose!
Yeah.
And that was supposed to be one of the charming attributes of the
Apparel Mart.
(She laughs.)
And I kept thinking well
the birds
undoubtedly are gonna drop on our food.
I have not been back to the Apparel Mart since.
(She laughs.)
I have no idea what they did with the bird shit.
So
everybody's all dressed up.
Very very excited
The
The reception
could *not* have been more enthusiastic
I mean there were
people *everywhere*
all over the airport
These streets of course were
were jammed.
And I read in the papers that Connolly had turned to Kennedy,
and said "Well Mr. President you certainly can't say that Texas
doesn't love ya."
People had in the hall, where we were waiting for him for lunch
had portable radios
listening to his progress in the motorcade

so kind of the word would be whispered from one table to the next
what point the motorcade had reached
and we heard, someone with a radio, that something had happened
people on the floor I saw were running up to the front where all
the dignitaries
We knew something was wrong.
Someone got to the podium
and I can't remember what they said,
the place was so buzzing
with people turning and looking and all kind of talking at once
And something was said that that
the President had been shot.
And um
and I know my first instinct was I had to get home.
I think that was the first instinct of almost everyone there.
(Blackout.)

HOUSE ARREST

ACT TWO

I. BIT BY BIT, DROP BY DROP

Slide: Alice Waters, Chef, Chez Panisse Restaurant

"PRESIDENTIAL PEACH"

Downstage center, carrying a peach, wearing a knit cap. In reality she is a "hip" white woman in her fifties from Berkeley, California.

He did come to Chez Panisse
(She giggles.)
Uhm
it was
electrifying for me.
I wanted him to
have a really good time here.
I knew I, that I couldn't make an impression on him in terms of food.
I knew that I couldn't
in that
in that period of time,
with just one time.
Because
uh uhm ah
I just think it's very hard for a public person
who doesn't eat well
to immediately
and I didn't want to force him into eating
what I wanted him to eat.
I put him in the back, behind the oven in the little corner
behind the booths,
and ate

every other tomato that I served him!
Just to make sure they were the most perfect tomatoes!
and he never ate one!
(She laughs.)
He never ate the tomatoes. *(She laughs again.)*
Uh
Well I had these lovely
little, orange
tomatoes that we had from the garden
and
and some homemade prosciutto
that was on the table
but they didn't eat that.
And he looked down the menu
And he wanted the blackberry ice cream
So we ultimately gave him that.
But it was a little bit of a dance,
I just kept bringing things
and when they ate it I would bring more
and just that kind of way.
I'm not even sure what all I brought him in the end.
I had thought
that I wanted to give him the one peach dinner
if he ever came to the restaurant.
I had sort of fantasized about that
'cause it's the most seductive
thing I could think of
and I would just give him peaches
in every form.
I would first
you know I would give him sliced,
and then uh maybe in a little,
Just a whole succession
of peaches.
So that he uh
but a great peach.
The best.
Just picked.

That one.
and I I
kept thinking he would really
he would understand something about peaches
and make transf
ANNA DEAVERE SMITH V.O. What about peaches?
ALICE WATERS. What about peaches?
Uh that when you eat a ripe one
when when you have a food
that it's just
uh
ripe and delicious and or just made well
you know like a bread that
just a great bread that just came out of the wood oven
and you you you,
I think people are transformed by that kind of
you know they they have that experience and it's just
one of those unforgettable things in their lives
and I just thought
if I could give him
some thing
that he would be
um
you know Georgia peaches
it's a Southern thing
it's a food he's used to and maybe he hasn't had a great one
and that somehow I could reach him.
(She hands the peach to someone in the audience.)

Graydon Carter, Editor of Vanity Fair

"WELL SHE WAS JUST GREAT"

Well, she she was just great, and and so I invited her
I mean not to be too
sort of cynical about this
but one of the things
you're supposed to sort of
uh
You're supposed to
you know
you're supposed to try to bring an interesting guest
to the thing.
And um
so Ellen DeGeneres is um
so.
I we asked her to this
and she said
yeah and I
thought well shit
they're she
they're gonna make a big splash because
Washington is a very conservative place.

Anonymous Man

"LAMBS TO DINNER"

*In reality a white man in his forties, a Washington "Insider."
He is wearing a tuxedo.*

*There is a long table, as at a big black tie dinner, with cham-
pagne glasses, ashtrays, half-eaten desserts, cups of coffee —
the final course of a long evening. Candles are lit on the table.*

Now you're invited to the table in Washington
and everybody loves
look at Anne *(Heche)* and look at Ellen* *(De Generes.)*
And it's like these *lambs* are brought to the dinner and they're
served up as *roast*.
I just thought the display was just so off-tune
knowing Washington and
knowing how it would be perceived
it was bowling alley.
It wasn't classy.
It was bowling alley.
It's been universally panned.
Gay you know
Gay groups are pissed off that they were so
you know, laissez-faire in their sexual attitude in front of the
President.

**This refers to a White House correspondents' dinner which Ellen De Generes
attended with Anne Heche.*

Graydon Carter, Editor of Vanity Fair

"DIDN'T BOTHER ME"

Smoking a French cigarette, wearing a tuxedo.

They were pawing each other a little too much at dinner for some
people
but uh
it didn't bother me.
Well,
they had their arms around each other the whole night
but it didn't bother me.
My staff thought it
might have
but it didn't at all.
Well, they thought
"Oh My God
poor Graydon
you know
Ellen and Ann are literally *fucking* on the chairs
and and right beside him in the dinner"
Basically I either didn't notice it that much
but it
it just didn't bother me.

Judith Butler

"A SCREAM"

In reality, a white lesbian academic, a scholar of rhetoric at U.C. Berkeley. Downstage of the table. Wearing a leather jacket.

It's a scream, I think it's all a scream.
I think really clearly
(Ellen and Anne) approaching the President with their arms
around each other
for the photo opportunity
in order to um to produce uh a sensationalist picture —
It doesn't strike me as
gay pride at its finest hour
if that's
what you're asking me. *(She laughs loudly.)*
For them to do that in that room
it's not as if they're they're entering
sexuality into the scene.
Hardly
Because where Bill Clinton is there's already sexuality in the scene.
So in some ways, all they're doing is exposing the subtext of sexuality that's already in the room.
I mean he could never do that with his sexuality.
He would
it's totally,
totally, unacceptable.
Evidently she has more
power than he does. *(She laughs.)*
'Cuz she can do something
he cannot do and in doing it
she exposes the fact that
he can't do it.

Anonymous Man

"WAY TOO ACADEMIC"

The same anonymous man as before, he is eating dessert robustly.

Too Academic
way too academic
Talking about something that Washington can't handle at all
Sex.
And any kind of sex.
But like *"gay sex?"*
Like,
because you know
it's it's just not part of the *game.*
It's not part of what you *say.*
It's not part of
It's a very tight WASP environment.
It's a very very enclosed
tubular environment.
You don't talk about depression.
You don't talk about foibles.
It's a town where you only talk about strength and manipulation,
and Machiavellian points of view.
So you don't let on weakness.
You know, if you say that you are,
have struggled
or are in *therapy*
with your wife
over your child's
drug addiction
you'd be ...
You wouldn't be able to run for President

today if you were in *therapy.*
Sex is so *dangerous*
Sex is so …
Look at the way people dress in Washington!
It's the most
sexless town!
Your your uh costume designer has to go really to *Papagallo's*
you know.
It's the most unsexy place.
Look at the way people dress at those dinners
you know
It's like they
they bought their stuff at
um
you know
at um
Loehman's.

Graydon Carter

"THAT ARC"

Carter lights another cigarette.

We went up to
I don't know, somewhere in the Hilton
and so the door comes in here
and there's all these people clusters of journalists
people getting awards and stuff
like that
and Ellen and Anne and George Clooney
and his girlfriend
and I are standing over here.
Well Clinton comes in and he just
you can see it in his eyes
his eyes
just work the whole room
He just locks in
he knows where he's going.
And he can't make it too obvious
and come right here
cause that's
Ellen,
George Clooney the whole thing.
Okay.
He wants to get over here as fast as he can.
Well he's on crutches.
And so he starts off like this
and somebody said
"Should we go over to him?"
I said "I will put money
he will be here in front of us in five minutes!"

Sure enough,
hobbling along,
saying hello to here
saying hello to there,
he just made
that arc so perfectly.
You know all these people are sort of cut out of
the thing
and boom —
He was there. *(slight pause)*
He looked great too.
I've never been invited to the White House for dinner
and I wouldn't want to insult them,
but I probably wouldn't go.
I'd rather stay in the city with my kids.
I I just probably wouldn't *go.*
Well, it's the most uptight place in the world!
I'm sure you can have a nice life there,
but I'd be just too terrified of,
if it's a all built on power
uh
like
if I lost my job tomorrow, I'd be
I'd be *unhappy*
but I certainly
this is
you know
it wouldn't ruin my life.
But I think if you lost your big job in Washington,
it's over.
You gotta leave.

II. SENDING THE CANARIES INTO THE MINES

Anita Hill, Professor of Law

"SLICK, DIRTY"

This section is set up with a long table that is bare. No covering. Metal. There are four table microphones set up, or one that can move up and down the table.

First of all,
they used that whole idea of an uh
polygraph test as a threat.
They said well will you take a polygraph test, Ms. Hill?
So we called their bluff
then they accused us of inventing it as though
it was our idea to start with.
Then they said it's a trick.
It was slick, it was dirty
And another thing that you might think about,
it was slick it was dirty,
But President Bush in many ways was protected from that dirt.

Maggie Williams, Former Chief of Staff to First Lady Hillary Rodham Clinton

"LIE DETECTING"

Maggie Williams in reality is a black woman in her early forties.

I don't know if you've ever taken one
Well
you know
it's like going to the electric chair*
(She laughs.)
I mean
they strap you,
in
and put things all over you,
little wires that are connected to
your arms
like a blood pressure thing
and uh
I mean I kept thinking you know the whole time
when I was taking the lie detector test
and you sit in a chair and you think,
"Now what did I do in my life to get to the place
where I'm taking a lie detector test?"
Uh
ya know,
I just
I just
ya know you just feel like a common criminal.
(She laughs.)
is what you feel like
is like a common criminal.
*She is referring to the Whitewater Hearings, in which she had to testify.

91

"WASHINGTON POLITICAL INSIDER"

Alexis Herman, in reality, was a light-skinned black woman in her late forties, with a slight Southern accent.

There was a real possibility that I wouldn't have gotten through
you know.
you know,
the feeding frenzy.
And then the funniest thing to me was that
somehow I was labeled a "Washington Insider."
That was really, you know
that was really funny to me.
I've always felt
you know
as a black woman,
you know,
you're on the outside looking in,
trying to bring down the walls,
bring down the barriers
to be in the room
to get to the table,
you know?
You know,
My daddy was very active during his life
You know,
He was the first black to sue the Democratic Party because they
wouldn't give him an
absentee ballot.
He just didn't take no for answers,
you know.
He wasn't a fiery man;

he was just steady and persistent,
you know?
But he had this quiet way of getting people out of trouble, you
know,
in the South when they would get arrested or folk would end up
in jail in the middle of
the night or these —
we call it police brutality now;
I don't know what the name was for it then,
but people used to always knock on his door in the middle of the
night to say so-and-so
has been put in jail;
can you come and get him out?
You know, he would show up in court sometimes to keep kids, you
know, from being
thrown in jail.
Their mamas were calling,
you know,
because during those days there wasn't any real justice, you know.
The courts were white people and all white juries,
but yet he could go and talk to the judge and somehow get these
kids out of trouble.
So that was just how he was,
you know,
and they used to have these meetings,
the NAACP and a sort of group around Mobile,
He was a ward leader.
The only ward in Mobile where people could go and vote was
Ward ten,
where my daddy was, like, the ward leader
Anyway, I used to ride in the car with him at night.
You know, my parents weren't married.
My mom was a single mom,
but he was a very good father to me,
and he would come and pick me up from school,
you know,
and take me riding in the evenings.
And if he had his business to do,

you know, he would ride, a
and I would go with him,
and I'd sit in those meetings,
you know,
and I'd sit over there with a coloring book or whatever;
but that's how he spent time with me.
So – and on Christmas Eve,
we always took these rides out,
you know,
and that's how he would put me to sleep and bring me back home.
So that's kind of what I did with him.
And this one Christmas Eve we were going over the bay to Father
Warren, he's a
priest,
and —
I was only five.
And we went for our ride,
and he went to one of his meetings over at the bay.
My daddy had a silver pistol with a pearl handle,
and he was a peaceful man.
I never heard my daddy curse or raise his voice a day in his life.
He kept his gun right here in the front of his old Desoto.
Green and white.
We had lots of Desotos
(But this one) was green and white.
But whenever there was *trouble,*
you know,
something was going *on,*
the gun came out from under here,
and he would always put it by his side.
Now, I used to like to sit up under my daddy when we would be
riding,
and sometimes,
you know,
how daddys put you in their lap and let you steer the wheel? But
if the gun was on the *seat,*
then I knew that there was a problem.
He didn't tell me,

but that was the symbol,
and I would always hug the window,
you know.
I guess I was scared.
I was scared of that gun.
I wasn't necessarily scared of what was going on outside because I didn't necessarily
understand it contextually, but I was scared of that gun,
you know.
(Louder.)
I didn't like that gun
because it was just a symbol of tension and something was wrong,
and my daddy could be hurt.
You know, it was more of that.
I knew there was a problem when he knew he had to have this gun.
I didn't want anybody messing with my daddy. So this particular night the gun is out, we
go over the bay, we go over to Father Warren's,
and they were all in their meeting.
And we get back in the car.
In those days, over the bay, dark roads, dirt roads, no lights, the church is way back off
the road.
And we're coming back from the meeting that night,
and, you know, the cars and the lights had come behind us, and my daddy starts driving
fast, and we're trying to get around these cars, and they're,
you know,
pushing us off the side of the road with the cars, and he's having —
(Responding to a question.)
It's the Klan, yeah.
So we're kind of wobbling all round the trees and stuff.
So eventually he had to stop the car,
and he was perspiring.
My daddy, you know, he was real calm,
but he was perspiring.
So he just stopped the car.
He pulled over,

just stopped,
and he said,
you know,
he said,
"Poppy's got to get out of this car,"
and he says,
"I'm going to put this gun in your hand,
and I want you to get right down there,"
and he pointed, like, under the dashboard.
And he said,
"You get down there,
and Poppy's going to put this gun in your hand."
And he says,
"I'm going to have to get out of this car,
and I'm going to lock this door."
He said,
"If anybody opens that door,
 I want you to pull that trigger."
And he took my finger and he put it right on that trigger and he
put that gun in my hand
and I had it just like this and I was down under the dashboard
(Responding to a question.)
Oh, yeah. I was tiny.
I was only five.
I was always a small child.
And that's where I got.
I got down–on–the-floor-underneath-the-dashboard by the seat
with the gun in my hand,
and he got out and locked the door,
and he just started walking to face the Klan.
And he told me
"Don't raise my head, don't look up, don't look out."
You know, I could hear him, you know.
I could hear them.
You know,
you could see the car lights and stuff, but mostly I could hear them.
What I remember more than anything were these sounds,
you know.

Yelling,
names,
and shouting.
I remember that more than anything.
That's why for years I didn't talk about this because I could hear
those sounds.
"Nigger," you know,
"get him, kill him, beat him,"
you know, just, just sounds.
I just remember — I remember "nigger" more than anything. What
I remember more than
Anything was just the word "nigger";
"Get that nigger."
"Here comes that nigger,"
you know.
So, anyway, I just remember "nigger" more than anything.
So it seemed like forever.
I really don't know how long it was,
but it felt like forever that I was down there with this gun, and
eventually
I heard Father Warren's voice saying,
"Alexis, it's all right.
It's all right.
I'm coming to the car.
Don't do anything. Don't do anything.
It's Father Warren.
I'm coming to the car.
I'm coming to the car."
And, you know, he got to the car,
and he opened the door, and basically —
see, they knew that it was trouble that night,
you know,
That's what they had been meeting on.
So they had followed my daddy because they didn't trust him to
get back to the city okay, like over the bay. So they had a little
posse that followed him, which they would do sometimes. But this
night they had made a decision to follow Poppy, so they followed,
and luckily they did.

So they roughed him up,
you know,
by the time Father Warren had gotten there.
But they took him on to the hospital and somebody came and drove me home.
Somebody drove me home. It might have been Father Warren. I don't remember.
They took my daddy wherever they took him because they had beat him up,
you know.
And then they took me home,
and I kind of remember seeing,
you know,
looking up,
and I saw them putting him in the other car;
Oh, his shirt was torn off.
I remember —
because my daddy was a neat man, too. That was the other thing, and I think for a child's impression, to see my daddy's white shirt torn off of him,
and he had straight black hair that he wore back,
and it was,
like, hanging all down around, you know.
And them carrying him.
I don't remember him being conscious.
And somehow to wear the mantle of a Washington political insider was just funny to me
you know
It was just funny to me.
ANNA DEAVERE SMITH V.O. You grew up in the south with the Klan, and had some personal run-ins with them. We don't have the Klan the way we did when you were a child. In a word, what do we have now?
ALEXIS HERMAN. You say, In a word?
You know, unfortunately,
almost the absence of the visible and the tangible
leaves the impression
that the problem isn't there,

that the issues are not there,
you know. And so I think what you have
is this false sense,
really,
now that everything is okay,
you know,
because you *don't* have the Klan.
So the flip side of that
is this immediate conclusion that it's no longer a problem, when it
still is.
And so I'm trying to figure how to say my feelings of it.
Oh, I can't say that on tape.

"MAKING A KIND OF A POLITICAL POINT"

But the uh
the test itself was horrible
and I thought, once I had taken it
"Well there
people will *have* to see
they'll *have* to see that
I'm telling the truth
and then of course by the time I had taken the second one and
passed it
I said "Well, you know, this is you know a hands down situation."
Nothing changed according to the
questioning and the treatment,
in fact it got harsher.
What they care about is making a kind of a political point
and then they really didn't care about me
I was just in the way.
I mean I switched it from being so intent
on trying to remember things
and get ready
for these things
to just reading the Bible
because it was clear that they didn't care about anything that I had
to say
ANNA DEAVERE SMITH V.O. Did you know that you were
going to Washington to fight?
MAGGIE WILLIAMS. Oh no
Oh no
I wasn't going to Washington to fight.
I was going to Washington
and I was going to work for the First Lady

because
I had just, I mean
my experience in having worked with her before
was
you know we had worked on, I thought the most important issues
there were.
We worked on children and family issues
and
if she was going to keep doing that
which I was sure that she was
to me it seemed like
you know the most important thing I could do
and she gave me such great hope,
quite frankly,
and that's what I thought I would be doing.
And
Uhm,
I didn't think that I would
be having to
defend my
integrity?
And,
Also the idea,
that you have people, chipping away,
at you know
this person that
you, and
your mother, and your father,
and all these other people have worked *so hard* to help
create —
And in an instant,
they can
uhm,
I didn't think
that I would be wasting so much
time.

"HOUSE ARREST"

I feel like I have,
a very limited space
and it's really limited to my physical home
but
just the house,
just the house.
To some extent I'm more at home in Norman, Oklahoma, than I
am any place.
It was just bizarre yesterday.
The first thing I did I went to
a place to get a cup of coffee,
and the the
woman behind the counter
said
"What-is-your-name?"
As though she was interrogating me!
As though I was some kind of an imposter.
She said
"Well I had heard that you hadn't lived in Norman in a long time"
and so
you know what I thought was my home in some ways has been
taken away from me by these *myths* that go around.
So even in the town that I thought was my home
I can't go in and be completely anonymous,
and completely relaxed.
I still have to
deal with the question about who I am and what I'm doing here.
I think that (home) is as much psychological and spiritual as it is
physical.
To the extent that I am at peace here now
it's not because this place has fulfilled the promises we thought it

would it's because *I* have fulfilled the promises and faced up to its limitations.

III. DARKNESS AT NOON

Slide: Ed Bradley, Sixty Minutes *Host*

"CAPTIVES"

In this section, the characters simply change ties — that is, each character has a different tie — or if one actor, or if there are fewer actors than narrators, a change of tie signifies a change of character.

ED BRADLEY. *Eating a carton of yogurt; shirt, tie, no jacket.*
(The press and the President.)
Both are captives.
Um
I think the press is
individually and collectively a captive
of the White House
(He puts a spoonful of yogurt in his mouth, and scrapes the cup.)
in that
you go there every day
and you stay there
(He scrapes the yogurt cup.)
The press is ushered in
for
a specific period of time
a minute, two minutes
so they can get a picture
they stand there with notes and pads
eh
"Mr. President what about Bosnia?"
Scream at him
If he wants

If he has something he wants to say then he'll use that opportunity
He'll take advantage of it.
If he doesn't,
Most of the time he'll ignore you.
Sometimes the President will say something
when he has no intention of saying something.
When it's not thought out,
and you get a free
something.
but it's really a very limited exchange.
He's a captive
because
He's there.
Uhm
It's a very
controlled existence.
Uh
There's no freedom.
You can't just pick up and go.
You can walk out here today and decide
Well let me run over to Barney's I need to pick this thing up.
The President to do that has gotta take an entourage,
Somebody's gotta go there with dogs,
and uh eh
ya know it just becomes uh you you
you are a captive of the White House.
True you have a lot of power and there's a lot you can do with it.
But you are a captive
And the press
is very much a captive
because
(Hits his hand on the desk along with the next line in rhythm.)
if he moves, we move
if he sits, we sit.
(Hits the desk again.)
And people don't like to say it
but everybody
particularly in those situations

and given the climate and the world we live in today,
everybody's on the death watch.

Slide: Christopher Hitchens, Journalist — The Nation, Vanity Fair

"SEX AND DEATH"

Drinking a scotch, and smoking. Hitchens at table with food that goes untouched. (In reality Hitchens is a white man in his early fifties with a British accent.) A sunny, nice restaurant in Washington on a corner.

But what impressed me from the start was this
it was his relationship between sex and death.
Death.
In the following way.
I went to New Hampshire
in ninety-*two*
for *Harper's Magazine*
um
and it was the week
of the Flowers
flap,
and I must say from her tapes and her press conference,
however those were manipulated by the *Star* or the *Enquirer* or
whatever it was,
It was fairly obvious to me
that she had been telling the truth.
And probably had been in love with the guy
and that therefore it couldn't be
between them,
well she says that and I say the other thing
He said
She said
never never actually really occurs.
Because if she's saying and it's not true

either I'm a liar
or she really is
a menace.
She'd have to be
wicked.
So that means you'd have to trash her,
to impute a bad motive
you can't get out of it.
What would a woman have to do to make a thing up
like that?
A lot
Clearly Flowers wasn't doing that.
Or so it seemed to me.
So that week,
Clinton was slipping in the polls
Clinton was expecting to win New Hampshire.
He actually never did.
He leaves the trail
goes back to Arkansas,
and supervises the execution of a mentally lobotomized
physically lobotomized,
There's a man called,
(*was* a man called)
Ricky Ray Rector
who had committed
who had indeed committed uh murder.
He was already quite disturbed
And having killed these people,
he put a gun to his own head and blew away his prefrontal lobe
and he was nursed back to life
so that he could be executed.
Uh but he knew no more about what he'd done,
had no conception of it
and the best
the most encapsulating anecdote of this is that,
he was well known to be say,
when they brought him his tray every night
his snack

in jail,
he'd always leave his dessert on the side
of the tray and eat it later
save it.
And on the night they came
they read him his rights —
they came to say well you've got to come now
(they don't gas them in Arkansas,
lethal injections)
He said okay,
I'm ready
but this is my pecan pie
I'm coming back for it.
And they realized then he didn't have any idea
what was happening to him.
So
I have heard people in the Clinton camp be asked,
then and since
"Just one question,
Would Mr. Rector be alive
if it wasn't for the New Hampshire primary?"
And say
"Well yeah he would be
okay I admit it"
Well I have no further questions.

"ARE YOU NOW OR HAVE YOU EVER BEEN"

Change of tie, puts on glasses.

And for the record I am keenly aware that I am being taped.
And not only I'm aware of it but I enthusiastically accept.
And so so
The day that Clinton first responded to the scandal
I guess it was a Wednesday
and I just remember just watching those interviews,
The Jim Lehrer interview and the Mara Liasson interview
and you know just watching so closely with my colleagues
you know every
you know every single verb tense,
uh you know
for example
I think
in one of the
interviews
Clinton kept saying
"I am not having an affair with Monica Lewinsky"
or "I'm not having an affair"
which of course would lay open another double entendre
the issue had he had an affair?
It's why in the nineteen-fifties the red hunters kept saying are you
now or have you ever been a member of the Communist party?
First of all,
of course I'm having a good time
I mean there was a moment in December January,
where I really was actively wondering whether I had made a totally
wrong career choice.
I mean here I am

growing up wanting to be a newspaper columnist,
and I really thought that how come all the good stuff like the Cold War
Joseph McCarthy, Vietnam happened on Walter Lippman's watch,
and I get Bill Clinton and the balanced budget?
Then suddenly we had this?
And all of life changed.
But, let's make no bones about it.
I mean
It doesn't get any better!
I mean this is life not only imitating art
It's doing *better* than art.

David Kendall, Attorney for President Clinton
re: Monica Lewinsky

"IS IS"

Sitting at a table in white linens, opening his napkin and beginning to eat soup. Jacket and tie.

I thought that the actual, that
if you could ever get anybody back to what he was
saying,
they would understand that it was not so silly — to say
"It depends on what the meaning of is is."
He was retrospectively parsing what his lawyer was saying.
His lawyer — was, there is no sex.
He said look,
And what he was asked,
"Wasn't your lawyer wrong
and misleading the court?"
he said "No,
it depends on what the meaning of is is."
What the President was saying was,
when my lawyer said there is no sex he had been speaking of the
present.
That was an accurate,
that was an accurate
quote.
If however he meant there had never been anything,
putting aside the meaning of sex,
if there had never been anything *amorous* there
he would have been wrong.
Again,
the President is very *smart,*
he is *analytic,*

and he can
make distinctions which are very fine.
There's nothing wrong with that.
People have held up "Depends on what the meaning of is is"
as if it was perfectly self-evident, always, in all contexts
what the meaning of is is.

Walter Shapiro, USA Today *Columnist*

"SPINACH DIP/SAD"

Coming back from Washington the night the Starr report came
out, having gotten from Kinko's copy shop.
It was kind of nice to just sort of be the center of attention at dinner with close friends and they would say something
 and I would say, "Not exactly. Let me show you footnote four
hundred thirty-two; the one about spinach dip."
But now
that we're in for the long haul with this
the whole thing
having now chortled about how wonderful it is,
The whole thing is sad.
The whole thing is sad.

Slide: Mike Isikoff, Investigative Reporter, Newsweek

"PERSISTENCE"

In reality Isikoff is a white male in his forties.

You have to be persistent.
I mean
people hang up on you
people slam doors in your face.
One thing you do have to have that's important,
particularly on this stuff
I don't know
you have to have a really thick skin.
Now you're putting me on the couch and I don't wanna go there.
I don't know
But for this story go back to *The War Room*
It was the shame card that they use,
"Serious journalists don't ask questions about *stuff*
like this. You're telling me you're a *tabloid* reporter?
You're asking me sleazy questions!"
Look at the way Mike McCurry describes me to Howie Kurtz in
Spin Cycle!
"That *sleazy,*" in the Kathleen Wiley thing,
"This other new *sleazy* charge being promoted by another *bimbo
beat* reporter Mike Isikoff
who goes around chasin' sex stories
how *cheap* and *tawdry,*
scum."
They'll think you're scum.
They'll make fun of you.
You're a bimbo beat tabloid reporter.
That's the way they use this to keep people off of
this stuff. *(Pause)*

There's a tawdry element to this stuff.
I just thought it was gonna be …
It was a story.
I thought that Clinton's private conduct was reckless,
and for the most part, most of these women were telling
the truth
and in that sense,
they were lying,
the Clinton people were lying and the women were telling the truth.

Chris Vlasto, ABC News Investigative Reporter

"THE BLUE DRESS"

Wearing a black leather jacket, and no tie (In reality Vlasto is a white male in his thirties, much more au courant than others in the play).

The — blue — dress.
Oh I knew about it the first day and nobody wanted to touch it before
before we broke it.
I had known that she,
I had heard that she had sent up a dress
that had semen on it
and
with all the gifts
to her Mother in New York.
And I thought it should have been mentioned the very first day.
But
"Oh,
we can't bring that up!
Oh come on Chris, shut up!
You cannot talk ...
We don't want to talk about *semen!*
Oh no!"
And they're goin' on and on
"You can't talk about *semen.*
Go awaaay."

IV. POLITICAL THEATER

Slide: The Grand Jury Testimony of the Forty-Second President of the United States, William Jefferson Clinton, by the Office of the Independent Counsel, August 17, 1998

A table is rolled out, and behind it sits the Rep. of the Office of the Indep. Counsel. Shirt, tie. No jacket. A microphone on the table, large stack of papers, a brief from the actual grand jury testimony.

OFFICE OF IND. COUNSEL. *(On a mike.)* If the person being deposed touched the genitalia of another person, would that be — and with the intent to arouse the sexual desire, arouse or gratify, as defined in definition (1), would that be, under your understanding then and now —

— sexual relations? Yes, it would? So, you didn't do any of those three things — Including touching her breast, kissing her breast, or touching her genitalia?

Would you agree with me that the insertion of an object into the genitalia of another person with the desire to gratify sexually would fit within the definition used in the Jones case as sexual relations?

I want to go over some questions again. I don't think you are going to answer them, sir. And so I don't need a lengthy response, just a yes or a no. And I understand the basis upon which you are not answering them, but I need to ask them for the record.

If Monica Lewinsky says that while you were in the Oval Office area you touched her breasts, would she be lying?

All I really need for you, Mr. President —

— is to say

— I won't answer under the previous grounds, or to answer the

118

question, you see, because we only have four hours, and your answers —

— have been extremely lengthy.

The question is, if Monica Lewinsky says that while you were in the Oval Office area you touched her breasts, would she be lying?

If Monica Lewinsky says that you used a cigar as a sexual aid with her in the Oval Office area, would she be lying? Yes, no, or won't answer?

If Monica Lewinsky says that you had phone sex with her, would she be lying?

Let me define phone sex for purposes of my question …

President William Jefferson Clinton

"BABY HUEY"

In the Oval Office, from an interview conducted with the President by Anna Deavere Smith, October 29, 1997. He wears a blue suit and shoes.

ANNA DEAVERE SMITH V.O. Do you think you are treated like a common criminal?
CLINTON. I think
George Washington
said he was treated sort of like a common criminal.
I don't know about that.
No I wouldn't say that.
But I think that in terms of the way,
uh uh a President
in the White House
even far more than Congress gets pilloried in the press.
The political press has this image,
that the presidency is so all-powerful
that none of the presumptions
should apply.
No presumption of innocence.
No presumption that some techniques
and things are off-
balance.
I think we really ought to ask ourselves,
Do we want to put our public officials in the position
of basically having to bankrupt themselves just to survive in office?
And I just think it's-gotten-out-of-whack.
I think that the thing is seriously-out-of-whack.
I was so naive that I really
believed them when they said

if you were honest and forthright
it would clear
the air.
I mean it's chilling when you really think about what happened.
(Speaking very fast and emotionally.)
When Hillary's
legal
uh bills were found
Oh it was all over the papers right?
She had to go talk to a grand jury.
First lady going to a grand jury.
Big pictures!
Now
What happened?
We said
We don't know where these came from but we're glad they turned
up because they support her story.
Why would we cover up records that support *her* story?
That was down in,
paragraph ten here.
Then what happened?
Another totally independent inquiry
by a Republican law firm
spent three-point-six million dollars
lookin' in to *all* the documents
on the savings and loan
you know what it said?
"*No* basis for criminal action
No basis for a civil suit
The records
support Hillary's account!"
Did all those people
who *blared* the record discovery?
Who *blared* the grand jury testimony?
All over America?
bother to tell the American people that
that's what this
report

done by a Republican law firm
after they spent almost
four million dollars said?
No!
(Intense, rapsy.)
Little bitty notice made!
So
what I'm saying is
Ya know, we're fine.
We're standing here.
We're showing up for work.
We're fine,
Bad for America.
Bad for the system.
Makes good people less willing to run.
And it corrupts the search for the truth.
Because,
the only target in town is the White House!
If Congress does this it's not so bad.
I told you what that Republican Senator told me —
and you can use this
He said
"Before you got elected we were stupid enough to think the press
was liberal
and then we realized"
He said "Then you got more grief that anybody had ever gotten
before
and then we realized that they are liberal in the sense
that most of 'em vote Democratic.
They vote with you but they think like us"
And when I asked him what he meant he said,
"You're a Democrat
You come here thinking you can do good.
You want to use the power of the government to make good things
happen to improve people's lives.
Republicans are *suspicious*
of the ability to make anybody's life better.
We like this because we have power

and the press
they want power.
So let 'em vote with you they think like us
When you're in
they get power
and we get power the same way.
We hurt you."
So never mind what the truth is,
hit the target.
Now
I just keep standin' up I'm like one of those old Baby Huey dolls
that we had when you're a kid.
You punch 'em and they come back up
So I'm fine.
But it's bad for the country.
It's bad when the system doesn't care
whether the attack is true or not.
It's bad when the burden of proof is on the accused,
and you're supposed to disprove,
all conceivable accusations,
present,
and future,
and if you don't,
there's something wrong with you.
It's bad when innocent middle-class people who work at the White
House
can be bankrupted
by
exorbitant legal fees
It's bad ...

V. MORAL SLIPPAGE

Slide: President George Bush, Sr.

"FAT, DUMB AND HAPPY"

From an interview conducted with the president by Anna Deavere Smith, Washington, D.C., Summer 1997.

ANNA DEAVERE SMITH V.O. We — probably don't think — I would say some behave as though maybe they don't think we need a President. *(He is drinking an orange crush and eating a chocolate chip cookie.)*

As long as the economy is good, everybody is fat, dumb and happy,
that may be right.
We might not need a President.
The economy goes down,
people get thrown out of work,
that will change.
I hope that doesn't happen.
But when the economy is good,
we say, hey, get the government out of my life.
I don't need it.
Who's the enemy any more?
Why do we need foreign policy
or ambassadors or all of this,
and you have voices of isolation from the right
to some degree yelling "Come home America" kind of thing.
And joined by big labor
ah, "We don't want to export our jobs."
And so you have a kind of an interesting coalition.

But as long as the economy is strong and people are happy, overall, you're not going to have a great worrying about the White
House.

"DOES A TREE MAKE A SOUND?"

In reality, Flip was a white man in his forties. Speaking very fast.

Norma McCorvey,
who's the Jane Roe of Roe versus Wade.
I can remember when I had the privilege of baptizing her,
I had the privilege of,
you know, leading her to Christ.
And what happened with Norma,
she's with us here,
and has been with us,
is here is Jane Roe of Roe versus Wade.
Sandra Cano,
of Doe versus Bolden,
those two cases that which legalized abortion, number one.
And then made it — Doe versus Bolden made it legal through all
nine months.
Both of those ladies,
Sandra Cano and Norma McCorvey, neither one of them ever had
an abortion,
never, and, and they were used by the abortion industry,
they were *used* by the abortion industry to bring these class action
suits.
Now both of them are confessing,
professing Christians that are doing everything they can to undo
the horror.
Well, what happened to them?
How did their politics change so much?
I mean, Jane Roe, let's face it,
was the spokesperson, the poster girl of the pro-choice movement.
But she jumped off the poster into the arms of Jesus.

What changes a person's politics is a change in the heart.
And that's what happened to me.
What changed all of my politics
and my whole world view
was that some new King got in my heart,
and the same new King got into Ms. Norma's heart,
and Sandra Cano's heart,
and in people's hearts all over this country.
And that's what's happening,
is the heart of the nation is changing,
but the laws are always lagging.
Laws always reflect the change in the heart.

ANNA DEAVERE SMITH V.O. Do you think America has a soul?

FLIP BENHAM. There's no question but that we have a spirit,
because that is what caused us to be so united,
I mean, the pilgrim forefathers that came over here.
Why was America reserved for the English?
Because they had the Bible!
Why not the French,
or at least the Spanish,
they had the Armada,
they were the great colonizers of the time,
not England.
But it was reserved for those people that had a *book*.
I mean, you look at this, and you find out,
what is the most quoted book of the founding fathers?
What book do they quote the most?
And their writings were voluminous.
And it's not like we, we hardly ever write.
It's the Bible.
you see, this is a forgotten book.
This is a book that nobody — I mean, it was forgotten by *me* for,
I didn't meet Jesus until I was twenty-seven years old, and I
thought this book was for people that needed a crutch.
As a matter of fact,
I thought Christians were people that committed intellectual sui-

cide in kindergarten and didn't know any better.
But I found out
I just
my eyes were open,
and I was *stunned.*
I was
I don't
I don't believe this yet.
And you see, what a psychiatrist couldn't do for me in a billion hours on his couch
spending bizillion of dollars for his counsel,
this book and this Jesus did in one divine moment in my life.
He turned my heart back toward home.
I was surrounded, north, south, east and west by me.
It was career, *my* life, *my* body, *my* rights, *my* choice.
Does that sound familiar?
"Not the church, not the state.
Women must decide their fate."
And you hear this *ranting* and *raving,* same world view.
And my one commandment is *(Angry.)* Thy shall not get in my face, don't you judge me, don't you dare judge me!
Nobody can judge me!
Then you look for the middle ground.
Can't we somehow find a middle ground here between the pro-lifers and those that believe in abortions?
The answer is, of course, you can't.
There isn't one.
Well, the answer is that you're going to be one or the other.
The answer is you are either going to convert like I did, like Ms. Norma did, or you're going to burn.
It's revival or death.
And that's the way it's always been, all through the history of the Bible.
In this country, most clearly manifested in the mid-19th century over the issue of slavery.
In other words, you will resist the evil,
even if it means that you're going to be punished by your government.
Because the government isn't God, God is God.

"A BABY FACE DOWN IN THE WATER"

Well, see
I don't think the law is necessarily about rightness and wrongness.
I mean, I think that's a large part of what the law tries to capture.
Um, but it also tries to capture obligations and responsibilities,
or weed out obligations and responsibilities.
So, you know, it's that terrible paradigm of,
you see a baby face-down in the water,
you don't turn it over,
did you commit murder?
No, our — our — our law says,
we're going to preserve that level of space for you and say, you have no, uh,
affirmative duty in this particular instance.
Um, even though it would have taken you *nothing*
and some states don't buy that,
and have passed good Samaritan laws, and others haven't,
and they struggle with how to deal with that.
I think the law tries to do right and wrong,
but also tries to preserve and protect certain freedoms.

"MIRROR TO HER MOUTH"

In reality Paulette was a very beautiful black woman in her
thirties wearing a simple, white tee shirt and jeans, no make-
up, hair pulled back.

I began to learn how to cover it up
because I didn't want nobody to know that this was happening in
my home
Ya know
I wanted everyone to think that we were a normal family
and I mean
we had all the materialistic things.
But that didn't make my children pain any less.
I ran out of excuses about how we got black eyes
and busted lips and bruises
me and the kids.
I didn't have no more excuses.
But it didn't change the fact that it was a nightmare
for my children.
It was a nightmare.
And I failed them
Dramatically.
Because I allowed it to continue on and on and on.
And that night that she got killed,
and the intensity just grew and grew and grew,
Until one night,
We came home,
from getting drugs,
and he got angry with Myeshia
and he started beating her.

And he just continued to beat her,
he had a belt he would use a belt,
I'm just speaking of the particular night that she died.
And he beat her
and he put her in the bathtub.
And I was in the bedroom.
but before all this happened
four months before she died,
I thought I could really fix this man
so I had a baby by him!
Insane?
Thinking that
if I give him his own kid
he'll leave mine alone.
And it didn't work.
We wound up with three children.
But the night that Myeshia died.
I stayed in the room with the baby.
And I heard him,
just beating her,
just beating her,
like I said he had her in the bathtub,
and every time he would hit her
she would fall.
And she would hit her head on the tub.
I could hear it.
It happened continuously,
repeatedly.
(Whispering.)
And I dared not to move.
I didn't move.
I didn't even go see what was happening.
I just sat there and listened.
And then later,
(She sucks her teeth.)
he sat her in the hallway
and
told her just set there

and she set there for 'bout
four to five hours
and then he told her to get up,
(Crying.)
and when she got up she said she couldn't see.
(Whispering, crying.)
Her face was bruised.
And she had a black eye.
All around her head was just swollen.
Her head looked like it was two sizes of its own size.
I told him let her go to sleep and he let her go to sleep.
(Whispering.)
The next morning she was dead.
He went on and checked on her for school.
And he got very excited.
And he said
"She won't breathe"
I knew immediately that she was dead.
'Cause I went in
I didn't even want to accept the fact that she was dead,
So I went and took a mirror to her mouth.
There
was *no* — thing coming out of her mouth.
Nothing.
He said
"We cannot let nobody know about this,
so you got to help me."
And I agreed
I agreed
I didn't dare tell anyone.
'Cause I had been keeping it a secret
for years and years.
And it just seemed like second hand to me
to keep a secret.
That night,
We went to the mall
and we told the police
that she had been missing.

We told like the security guards of the mall
that we had like lost her.
Ya know we fabricated this story and I went along with it.
And we told him that she had been missing.
But she wasn't missing.
So after that
we left the mall
and we told them what she had on
that night.
We got her dressed in the exact same thing
that we told the police that we had put on her.
And we got the baby
and we drove like out to
(Hear her getting the slightest bit tired here.)
I 95.
I was so petrified
and so numb
all I could look
was in the rear view mirror.
and he just laid her right on the shoulder of the highway
My own chile.
I let that happen to.

Slide: Brian Palmer, Photographic Journalist

"GETTING BEATEN UP IN AN ALLEY"

Putting his camera away into his camera bag.

ANNA DEAVERE SMITH V.O.   Right. Would you — would
you — did you ever think of a dilemma, the dilemma of being in
this position where you could save the President's life or take the
picture? Which one would you do?
PALMER.   If it came down to me,
I mean,
I would like to think that I would
I mean,
I would obviously sort of make the choice to assist a human life.
A human whether it's a
I mean, it doesn't really
it wouldn't matter if it was the President.
I mean,
if it's someone getting beaten up in an alley
and there's something I can do about it,
I'm not going to stand there and take a picture of it.
I mean,
I've been in situations in New York,
in street situations
where I've perhaps, unwisely,
you know, intervened
and I've had my colleagues say,
"Yeah, you know,
you're here to take the picture.
You're not here to get involved."
I would like to think that
if I feel that it comes down
to a point where I can save,

you know, a person or keep a person from getting hurt unneces-
sarily,
I would intervene.
I mean, if it's
I mean,
in situations where you can't do anything,
like people with guns who are fighting each other
I mean, if you step in between you get dead.
So, in those situations,
I would probably hang back and try to document
and then at least you would have that,
you know, sort of historical record of that event happening.
But I don't know. (Pause.)
I mean,
I'm always — I mean,
I've thought a lot, a lot, a lot about this.

VI. ONE CARD AT A TIME

Blese Canty, Church Member

"RIGHT BY THE ROPE"

In reality Blese was a black man in his late seventies in the South. Wearing work pants and a work-shirt.

(*Speaking slowly.*) Well
that was exciting day,
It was people from far off
and narrow,
They were here
Because
it just coincident
that the President
of the United State [*sic*]*
would come
to a little small town like
Greelyville.
There's very few people know where
Greelyville at.
Very few people know where
Greelyville at.
And that why it was such
a exciting
that
the President to come here to
Greelyville
A lot of people didn't believe
that it woulda never happened

* *Clinton went to visit Southern churches that were burned down in '96.*

136

And some of 'em come just to
really see
is that the
President himself?
or his
Vice President
or some of his workers?
But no this was the President
himself.
Well you know,
They had it barricaded off
and they had a rope around
so you couldn't get to him.
But otherwise we woulda
been about that far apart.
He wasn't way over yonder
and I way over here.
And I shake his hand
He say "How you doin'?"
I say "I'm doin' fine."
I say "I'm happy for you
I glad I glad to see
glad for you to be here today
I'm glad to see you."
This is the first time I've seen a
President face to face.
I never have shake a President hand
never have look a President
in the eye in all my days.

Studs Terkel

"COMMUNICATION"

In a trench coat with a cane, wearing Hush Puppies.

Moral Slippage, that was a phrase coined by Jeff Magruder.
He was one of Nixon's boys.
Jeff Magruder was one of Nixon's boys and he went to jail.
If it goes along without being challenged.
You see?
It becomes big then.
Sometimes it's drop by drop and bit by bit and we accept it daily
now more and more.
A thoughtful citizenry is what it's all about.
Now things are getting rougher and rougher because of the tech-
nology.
So this goes to the old fashioned phrase, it's hard, it's tough.
Grassroots.
See the cards are stacked
Now how do you unstack this particular deck?
It's a hard job.
It's gotta be one card at a time.
Grassroots is an old fashioned word
that did with personal contact
door to door
person to person
So I can tell you of another funny
playlet
The Atlanta airport is a modern airport.
And as you leave the gate,
there are these trains.
That take you to the
uh

concourse
and out to a destination.
You go on these trains
and they're smooth and
quiet and efficient and there's a voice you hear on the train.
The voice you know was a human voice.
See in the old days you had robots.
The robots imitated humans.
Now you have humans, imitating robots!
So you got this voice
on this train
"Concourse One
Dallas
Fort Worth Concourse Two
Omaha
Lincoln"
Same voice
Just!
as the train is about to go,
a young couple
rush in.
And they're just about to close pneumatic doors?
And that voice
without-losing-a-beat says
"Because of late entry we're delayed thirty seconds"
Just then,
everybody is looking at this couple
with hateful eyes
the couple is going like this shrinkin'.
And
said "Oh My God!"
I'd happened to have had a few drinks,
before boarding
I do that
to steal my nerves.
And so
I
imitate a train call

holding my hand
over my
"George Orwell,
your time has come!"
Everybody laughs when I say that
but not on that train!
Silence!
And they're lookin' at me
And so suddenly I'm shrinkin'!
So there I am with the couple
the three of us
at the foot of Calvary
about to be up'd you know.
Just then I see a baby,
a little baby in the lap of a mother,
I know it's Hispanic cause she's was speakin'
Spanish
to her companion
about a year old
a little baby with a round little face ya know
and so I'm going to talk to the baby.
So I say to the baby,
holding my hand over my mouth 'cause
my breath may be a hundred proof!
So I say to the baby
"Sir or madam
What is your considered opinion
of the human species?"
And the baby looks
you know the way babies look at ya
clearly
and starts laughing
busting out with a crazy little laugh
and I say
"Thank God
A human reaction!
We haven't lost yet!"
And so there we have it!

But the human touch
that's *disappearing* you see
So we talk about define
There ain't no defining moment,
for me
All moments are defining and add up!
There's an accretion of movement that leads to where we are now,
in which trivia becomes news
In which more and more less and less awareness
of pain of the other.
So this is an interesting dilemma with which we are faced.
I don't know if a used this or not,
I was quoting Wright Morris
this writer from Nebraska
"We're more and more into communications and less and less
into communication!"
So there you have it!
So okay kid!
I've got to scram.
I gotta go see my cardiologist!

End of Play

PROPERTY LIST

Martini (GEORGE STEPHANOPOULOS)

Stool (CINDER STANTON, ROGER KENNEDY)

Rocking chair (KEN BURNS)

19th-century writing desk, writing pen, liquor bottle (JAMES
    CALLENDER)

Candles (JAMES CALLENDER, ANONYMOUS MAN)

Coffee cup (ROGER KENNEDY)

Mimosa drink (ANNETTE GORDON REED)

Blackboard and chalk, 18th-century manuscript (THOMAS
    JEFFERSON)

White linens, napkins (RW APPLE, DAVID KENDALL)

China, wine glass with white wine, Indian hors d'oeuvres, menu
    (RW APPLE)

Reading glasses (RW APPLE, WALTER SHAPIRO)

Easy chair (WALTER TROHAN)

Ingredients to make biscuits, papers for unbound diary (LIZZIE
    McDUFFIE)

Rocking chair (replica of chair Lincoln was in at Ford's Theatre
    when he was assassinated), hand-held microphone, 19th-
    century coffin, American flag, 1865, a gun, 1865
    (PRESIDENT ABRAHAM LINCOLN)

Dress dummy with dress for Mrs. Mary Todd Lincoln, pins, pin
    cushion

Photo bag, light meter, film to load in camera (BRIAN
    PALMER)

Bunch of lilacs (WALT WHITMAN)

Desk, swivel chair (BEN BRADLEE)

Big chair (GLORIA STEINEM)

Elegant chair (GOV. ANN RICHARDS)

Peach (ALICE WATERS)

Long table (ANONYMOUS MAN, ANITA HILL,
    CHRISTOPHER HITCHENS, DAVID KENDALL)

Champagne glasses, edible dessert, fork, plate, spoon, cups of
    coffee (ANONYMOUS MAN)

Ashtrays (ANONYMOUS MAN, CHRISTOPHER
    HITCHENS)

French cigarettes (GRAYDON CARTER)
Four table microphones (ANITA HILL)
Yogurt and spoon (ED BRADLEY)
Scotch and glass, cigarettes, plate of uneaten food, fork, knife, napkin (CHRISTOPHER HITCHENS)
Soup, bowl, spoon, napkin, glass of water, bread (DAVID KENDALL)
Large file or lawyer's brief, microphone on a small stand or table (PROSECUTOR)
Wedding ring (PRESIDENT WILLIAM JEFFERSON CLINTON)
Orange Crush, chocolate chip cookie (PRESIDENT GEORGE BUSH, SR.)
Cane (STUDS TERKEL)

SOUND EFFECTS

Note: The sound design can be as simple or complex as is affordable.

Restaurant ambience, laughter
Music, a loud clock
Music: "Stars and Stripes Forever"
Gunshot
Party noises